Timeless Tropical

ORO *editions*

Timeless Tropical
Selected works by Timur Designs

Contents

006	*Foreword*
008	*An Introduction to Timur Designs*
010	*City Living*
012	Conservation House at Holland Park
022	Detached House off Holland Road
030	Detached House at Mount Echo Park
038	Conservation Townhouse at Cairnhill Road
044	Detached House at Vanda Avenue
050	Semi-detached House at Meyer Road
054	Terrace House at Makepeace Road
062	Apartment at Chay Yan Street, Tiong Bahru
068	*Waterfront Living*
070	Arrival Plaza, Sentosa Cove
080	Sentosa Cove House One
088	Sentosa Cove House Two
094	Sentosa Cove House Three
100	Sentosa Cove House Four
106	Sentosa Cove House Five
114	Beachfront Facilities at Palawan Beach, Sentosa
122	*Appendix*
124	Other Projects
127	Timur Designs
128	Photo Credits

006 | Timeless Tropical

Foreword

By Wong Yunn Chii, (PhD)
Head, Department of Architecture
National University of Singapore

The works of Timur Designs are visually delicious and experientially sensual. The skillfully framed photographs and carefully crafted texts in this monograph remain pale surrogates for the reality of their created settings. Their works should be experienced in real life. I say this with confidence, as I have been a beneficiary of many wonderful gatherings and meals in the houses of these very good friends over the years. Under the balmy tropical evenings in a garden pavilion or on a verandah, and over a fine spread of their wonderfully prepared home-cooked meals, the totality of architectural experience, mildly put, is fulfilled.

Leaving these personal ruminations let me stake out the other more serious aspects of Timur Designs' architectural offerings.

In 2004, Ai Loon and Wai Kin, the principals of Timur Designs were among a select group of twenty talented architects in Singapore nominated for the inaugural Urban Redevelopment Authority's *20 Under 45* Architects exhibition. The nominations were carefully reviewed by the Board of Architects, the Real Estate Developers' Association of Singapore, National University of Singapore and the Singapore Institute of Architects. The exhibition recognized their personal creative accomplishments as well as the their potentiality for greater works. And the works that Timur Designs has done since, as documented in *Timeless Tropical*, abundantly demonstrate their progressive achievements.

Thus, the question now to ask is: What exactly is being demonstrated in *Timeless Tropical*?

Firstly, there is an obvious evidence of a highly refined craft and sensitivity in house building for the tropics. Timur Designs attributes this to the traditional wisdom(s) of the "Tropical Asian" house. They have cast this regional influence with humility, but naturally there is more in their reflections. Their genre of architecture arises as much from the new lifestyle demands of urbane clientele who want to stay connected with natural surroundings. In this sense, by accepting the modern imperatives, Timur Designs has vernacularized the modern idiom in space, spirit and material. As such, they have successfully eschewed modernizing the vernacular forms; and instead, taken new cues from them.

Secondly, and this connects to the previous point, there is an emergence of a very productive integrative design approach which creatively reconstitutes outdoor and in-between spaces in the tropics. Timur Designs sees it fit to transform the outside of the house into a positive livable domain. In land-scarce Singapore, and possibly in many other build-up urban areas of Asia, these are vital strategic moves. They magnify the potentialities of extant spaces, as well as alter perceptions on how to do more without the excesses of more space.

Thirdly, by extending the sensibilities of the first two points, there is a promising new front towards tropicalizing public urban spaces. Here, we are offered a snippet of an urban space of slow pace to stem the accelerated time of our active city. Although the Palawan Beach (Sentosa) is the only one public commission proffered, we look with anticipation to future, larger ones. Hopefully, such opportunites will enable them to bring their domestic sensibilities to the public, just as they have brought their urbane sensibilities to the house form.

At the end of the day, what is to be learned from *Timeless Tropical*?

Beyond the labels of "new tropicality," "neo-tropical" and "zen tropical" that have been widely hyped to identify various trends of architecture in the tropics, we now recognize through the works of Timur Designs that "timeless" is actually timely. ***Timeless*** Tropical, simply put, is timely tropical because their works show us how to obtain the best out of the material and spatial settings in the tropics by creating a low energy and sensual architecture that befits the sustainability mantra of our age.

An Introduction to Timur Designs

By Chan Wai Kin and Yong Ai Loon

Timur
Timur is the Malay word for East. It is in this particular part of the world where many unique cultural forms thrive, and such customs and traditions in turn dictate traditional building forms. At Timur Designs, we choose to look towards Timur, the East, to inspire and shape our distinctive form of tropical architecture.

The Tropical Asian House
The fundamental essence of the contemporary Tropical Asian House traces its origins to the traditional and vernacular tropical house.

A notable example is the Malay house which is typically a timber house raised on stilts with large pitched roofs and ample window openings all around. The form of the house clearly reflects the way of life of its inhabitants. The interplay of hierarchy of public with private spaces dictates the house's layout starting from the *serambi* (guest verandah) which acts as a transition point between the public and private domains to the *rumah ibu* (core house) and then to the *dapur* (kitchen).

The Malay house is a home that is designed with a deep understanding of the climate and the environment. These vernacular buildings recognise the need to shelter users from intense sunlight and torrential tropical downpours, to control the glare from open skies and to ensure there is adequate natural vegetation in the surroundings to cool down the microclimate. This is evident in the ample openings in the form of windows, grilles and open interiors that provide effective ventilation throughout the house.

In this respect, the Malay house is no different from the Thai house or the Balinese house. The stylistic expressions may be starkly different, but at its core, it is the same tropical Asian house. To truly understand the tropical house, one must venture beyond the superficial.

Timeless Tropical
The traditional tropical house plays a crucial role in our perception of a home and living in the tropics. Tropical living usually occurs in the in-between spaces i.e. the spaces between the outdoors and indoors where there is sufficient shelter from the harsh climate, but also sufficient openness to relate to the outdoors. The fluid line between the outside and the inside draws the experience of the external into the interior. We usually find such spaces more lived-in compared to purely internal spaces.

Usually the client's brief focuses on the internal spaces. They seldom mention the external spaces except for built elements such as the pool. Timur's approach to interpreting their brief is to look at the design of the whole site and not merely the building. We go beyond conceiving the building as merely a box, and design the house as an ensemble of internal and external spaces that are engaged in intimate dialogue.

The layman might often be more concerned with "What does the building look like?". Whilst it is tempting to design architecture as sculpture, we believe that it is just as important to understand what the building feels like. It is more relevant to design living spaces that feel cool as opposed to building a pure glass box which must be perpetually shaded with blinds in order to make it livable. We want people to enter our buildings and discover the joys of surprising views and connectivity of spaces both horizontally and vertically, and to ultimately realize that there is more to architecture than just the physical appearance of the building.

The houses that Timur designs cannot be fully appreciated just from their externally appearances. With this book, we hope to invite readers into our houses and experience true tropical spaces as interpreted by us.

Timur makes it a point to fully comprehend what the client wants so as to deliver that personal touch and more. After all, a building must be much more than instant gratification and the glorification of the built form. We appreciate that a building has a unique life span during which the occupants will live, work, use and inhabit its every space. Guided by this understanding, we consistently aim to ensure that the building is as much about ease of use and adaptability, allowing the occupants to imbue it with their own character and stamp it with their own personality with every passing moment.

Inspired by the best time-tested tenets of tropical architecture that have been exemplified by the traditional Malay house and the British colonial buildings in this region, Timur strives to produce contemporary architecture that respects the climate, nature and the occupants. It is an architecture that we hope will continue to be relevant and timeless.

City Living

Conservation House at Holland Park

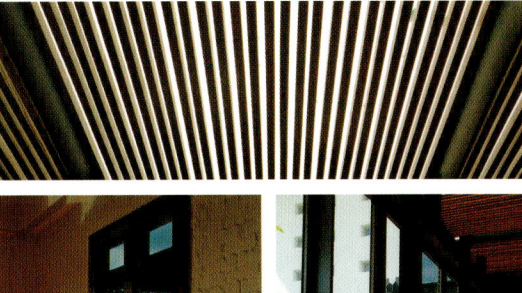

This existing Art Deco house has been gazetted for conservation by the Urban Redevelopment Authority (URA). The original main entrance faces away from the main gate of the newly sub-divided plot of land. The challenge was to layout the new additions to the conserved house in such a way that a new formal entry is created between the existing house and the new block.

This was achieved by inserting a new living room between the conserved house and a large existing tree, at once creating two intermediate elements with a character of their own: the main entrance porch adjacent to a pond, and the new timber deck onto which the living room space flows out to.

On the opposite side of the conserved house, a new bedroom wing was added, with the carporch below. This formed a new informal family entrance to the house with a direct connection to the service zone and the bedrooms on the upper floor.

The original house was opened up as much as the URA would allow in order to connect the house with its surrounding garden and new pool. Such a gesture makes the new complex, which comprises three blocks, more tropical.

The architecture of the new additions deliberately departed from the original Art Deco look in order to clearly identify what is old and new. However, the entire house was unified by careful integral planning, which included replicating the visually prominent horizontality of the ledges.

Conservation House at Holland Park | 013

previous page panoramic view of the three main components of the house: the conserved portion at the centre is flanked by the new living room on the left and the new bedroom wing on the right. the pool links the three sections together visually. *clockwise from top left* view of the new bedroom wing from the road; new entrance porch links the conserved house with the new living room; beyond the entrance porch, the new living room opens up onto a pond and a large timber deck under an existing tree; the new bedroom wing with the carporch below, replicating the horizontal lines of the concrete ledges in the conserved house; view of new entrance porch from the main gate. *opposite page, right* view of the corridor linking the conserved house to the new living room from the swimming pool. *far right* the balcony of the existing house has been enclosed to form the master bathroom.

014 | Timeless Tropical

opposite page, far left the new double volume living room. *left* the living room extends spatially to an external timber deck which wraps around an existing tree. *above* view of the interior of the conserved house; the existing concrete arch was accentuated by hacking away the brick infill walls around it.

Conservation House at Holland Park | 017

above the new spiral staircase highlights the lateral link between the conserved house and the new bedroom wing. vertically, it provides the linkage from the family room on the second storey to the roof terrace. *opposite page, far right* the new bedroom at the end of the swimming pool. a new timber balcony was added to the conserved house to open up the master bedroom on the upper floor to the pool below. *floor plans* the conserved existing house is in shaded grey, flanked by two additional new wings.

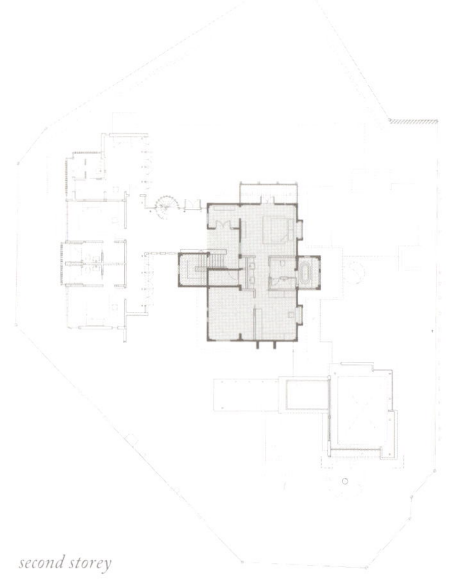

second storey

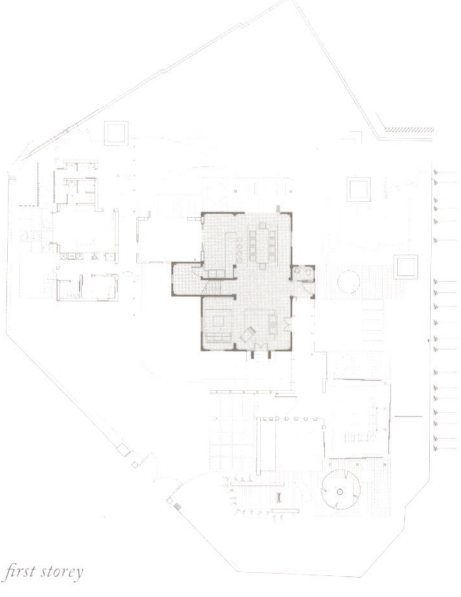

first storey

opposite page, top row landscaping to unify the new and the old. *opposite page, bottom row* the new link between the conserved house and the new living room is a glass enclosure with a trellis roof. its transparency accentuates its role as a negative space between the two main components. *top row* the existing staircase in the conserved house was retained. plastering on the existing wall was hacked off to expose the brickwork texture; as the stairs ascend to the second floor, walls were removed and metal railings added to give the house a lighter feel. *bottom row* new shelves act as railings on the second storey

Conservation House at Holland Park | 021

Detached House off Holland Road

The original house sitting on this piece of land was on the higher level while the pool was situated at the lower level, about four metres below. The new house was designed to integrate these split levels, such that the various levels provide a range of experiences as the occupant of the house moves around this compound.

The main bedroom wing of the new house is elevated above the covered verandah links, the carporch and the main entrance to the house. This elevated form is presented as the frontage and serves as a visual connection between the split levels of the house.

The deep, brick-clad piers on which the bedroom wings sit on is partially submerged in a reflecting pool. This creates a touch of formality to the experience of arriving and entering the house. The overflowing effect of the reflecting pool adds an element of motion to the otherwise static connection between the two split levels.

A series of internal and external staircases result in several spatial surprises, such as the 'hidden' poolside powder room which has direct access to the swimming pool from the shower cubicle. The internal spaces of the house are also located on a few split levels to further enhance the myriad of experiences that one can derive from walking around the house.

Timber is used extensively in the house design and frames all the openings in the external walls. This makes the envelope totally porous and tropically appropriate. Old railway sleepers from Malaysian railway tracks were imported and used here in a variety of ways such as garden paving, outdoor benches and garden bollards.

The old house was fully demolished but the old Chinese bricks were salvaged and recycled for the cladding of some feature walls in the new house. New fairface bricks were used to complement the recycled bricks on these walls.

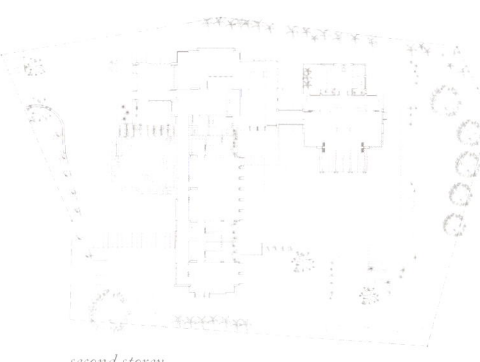
second storey

first storey

basement

024 | Timeless Tropical

previous page view from the pool at the lower level, with the living room on the right opening out towards it. the timber columns in the water support the master bedroom balcony above. the double volume pool deck area with brick-cladded columns is the transitional space between the lower pool area, the driveway and carporch at the upper level. *opposite page* close-up view of the feature walls, with the granite stairs cantilevering off the wall. the two walls, cladded in contrasting old bricks and white granite, are sheared to enclose an external staircase. under the staircase is the outdoor powder room and poolside shower. *above, left to right* the front of the house, behind the privacy screen which "wraps" around an existing mature mango tree that becomes a visual focus for all the spaces surrounding it; front façade of the house. the white granite-cladded feature wall acts as a privacy screen, with a small cut-out doorway for access into the house.

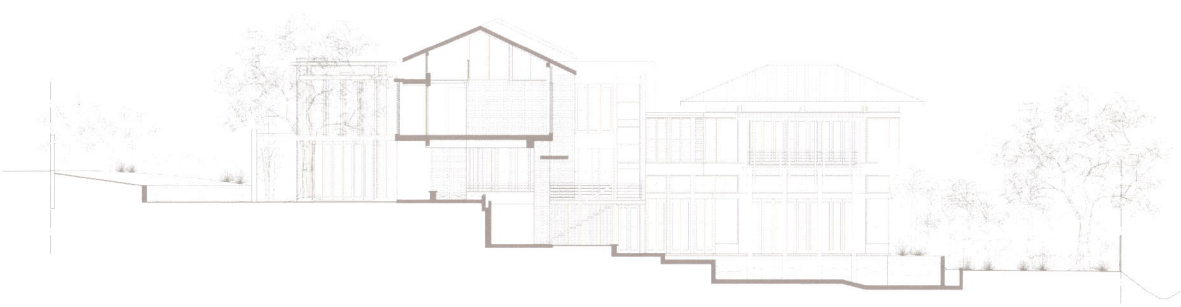

Detached House Off Holland Road | 025

left panoramic view of the house from the lower pool area. one of the two feature walls on the left is cladded with old chinese bricks salvaged from the old house when it was demolished, while the other is cladded in white granite. *right, top row* the master bedroom and living room pavilion, seen "floating" on the swimming pool; view of the main house and the pool from the master bedroom balcony. *bottom* view of the master bedroom cum living room pavilion linking to the main house, with the pool in the foreground.

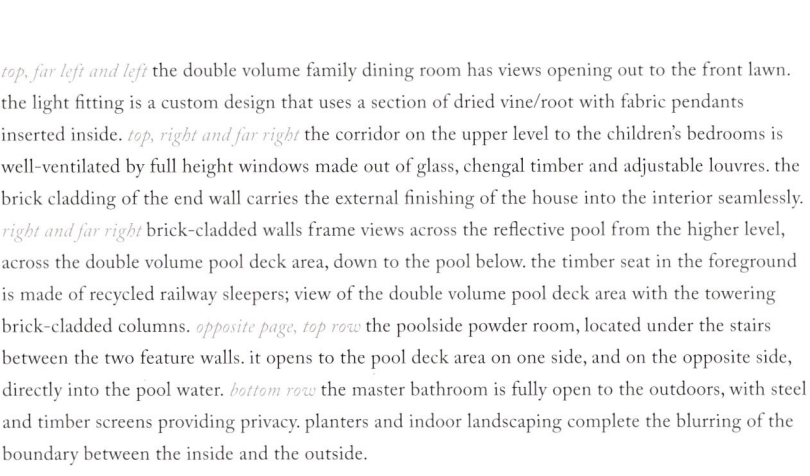  

top, far left and left the double volume family dining room has views opening out to the front lawn. the light fitting is a custom design that uses a section of dried vine/root with fabric pendants inserted inside. *top, right and far right* the corridor on the upper level to the children's bedrooms is well-ventilated by full height windows made out of glass, chengal timber and adjustable louvres. the brick cladding of the end wall carries the external finishing of the house into the interior seamlessly. *right and far right* brick-cladded walls frame views across the reflective pool from the higher level, across the double volume pool deck area, down to the pool below. the timber seat in the foreground is made of recycled railway sleepers; view of the double volume pool deck area with the towering brick-cladded columns. *opposite page, top row* the poolside powder room, located under the stairs between the two feature walls. it opens to the pool deck area on one side, and on the opposite side, directly into the pool water. *bottom row* the master bathroom is fully open to the outdoors, with steel and timber screens providing privacy. planters and indoor landscaping complete the blurring of the boundary between the inside and the outside.

028 | Timeless Tropical

Detached House Off Holland Road | 029

Detached House at Mount Echo Park

What was once a box-like house sitting on a large piece of land is now a light-filled structure which optimises its setting by providing high transparency between the interior and lush garden surroundings.

The original two-storey detached house had an inward-looking, bulky form. The additions and alteration works to the original house revised this spatial layout to create more connection to the garden and external spaces.

The architectural expression of the house was transformed by redefining the façade. Walls were opened up and shading trellises and roofs were installed to enunciate a tropical weather-proofing sensibility. A new entrance was created with an entry walkway over a reflecting pool and shaded by timber-slated screens. A feature staircase in timber and steel is cantilevered over the reflecting pool in a transparent double-volume space.

Timber deck terraces flanked by large koi ponds wrap around the living and dining spaces thereby extending the living area into the semi-open. These spaces look down onto the pool and garden on the lower level with the focus on a new timber pavilion by the end of the pool.

A new wing was introduced to contain a study and an additional bedroom on two floors. Both of these spaces have views out to the garden from three sides which can be opened with large timber doors and windows. A soaring timber roof caps the extension space above with a lightweight steel and timber structure.

previous page new pavilion and outdoor terraces flank the swimming pool and garden. *left* walkway to new entrance over reflecting pool. *above* contrast of shadows and light cast by carporch roof. *opposite page, top and bottom* large granite slabs hover above reflecting pool. *far right* slatted screen over reflecting pool provide shelter to the entrance area.

Detached house at Mount Echo Park | 033

second storey

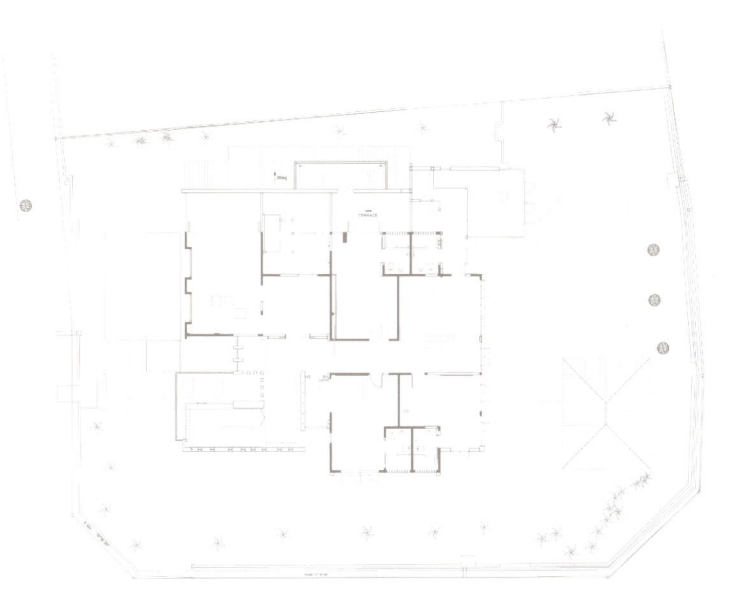

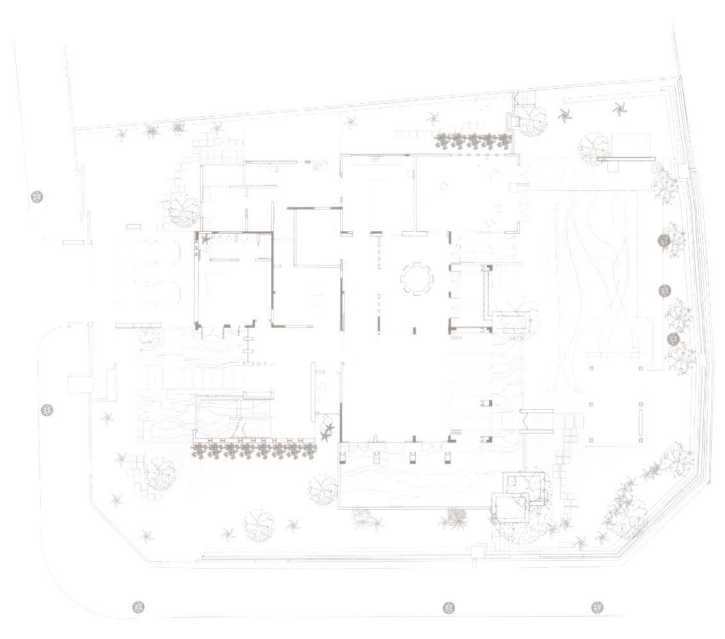

first storey

opposite page lush landscape and water features provide a soft contrast to granite and steel elements. *left* large slatted trellis provide shade and shelter to second storey openings.

Detached house at Mount Echo Park | 035

036 | Timeless Tropical

opposite page terraces outside living and dining areas lead down to pool. *left* staircase hovers over reflecting pool that extends from the outside to the interior of the house. *middle* staircase is bathed in natural light from slit openings in the feature wall. *right, top and bottom* bedroom in new extension looks out to the flourishing trees in the garden; the master bathroom opens onto an intimate, landscaped courtyard.

Conservation Townhouse at Cairnhill Road

This is a pre-war terraced house with the front sections gazetted as conserved. Typical of the colonial genre, the site is narrow and deep, with the length of the house punctuated by two internal courtyards which allow light and air into the internal spaces.

The most significant expression of this house is a new three-storey extension at its rear. This is a transparent volume which contains the master bedroom and study on the second and third storey respectively. Both these spaces are linked by a double-volume glass void which looks out onto a majestic rain tree. They are detached from the party walls and the narrow gaps are planted with lush greenery for an all-round pavilion-like feel to the rooms.

The new extension is linked to the conserved section of the house by a courtyard which has a soaring granite-clad wall that plunges into the koi pond below. The courtyard is covered with a rectractable skylight which makes the spaces below usable in all weather conditions. An open staircase that overlooks the courtyard is anchored around a feature wall painted a bright, fire-engine red.

Bathrooms are located along the side of the courtyards and are ventilated through vertical timber louvres.

The rooftop terrace over the rear extension is an outdoor living space that provides a reprieve from city living with a garden set under the canopy of the adjacent large rain trees.

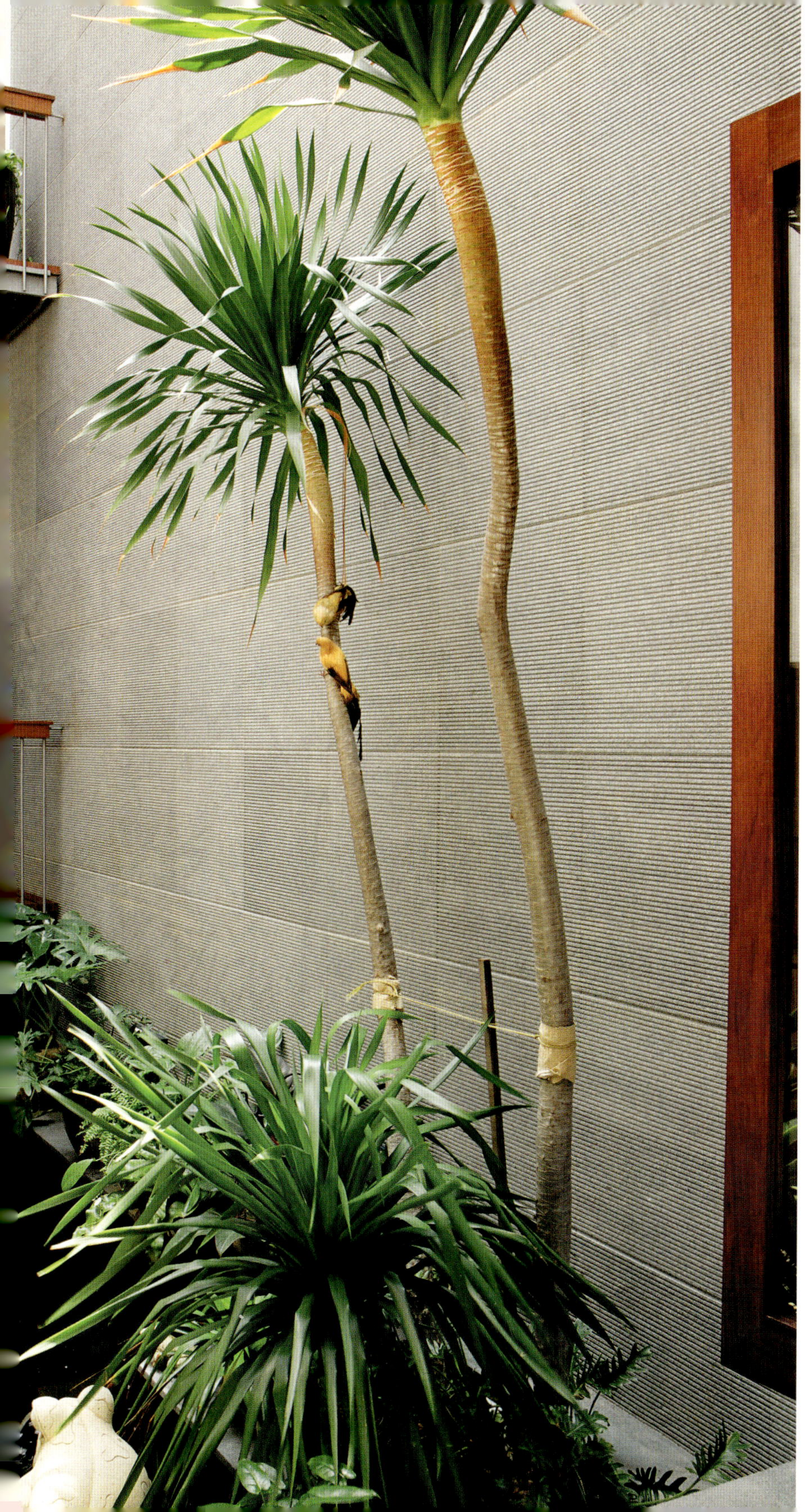

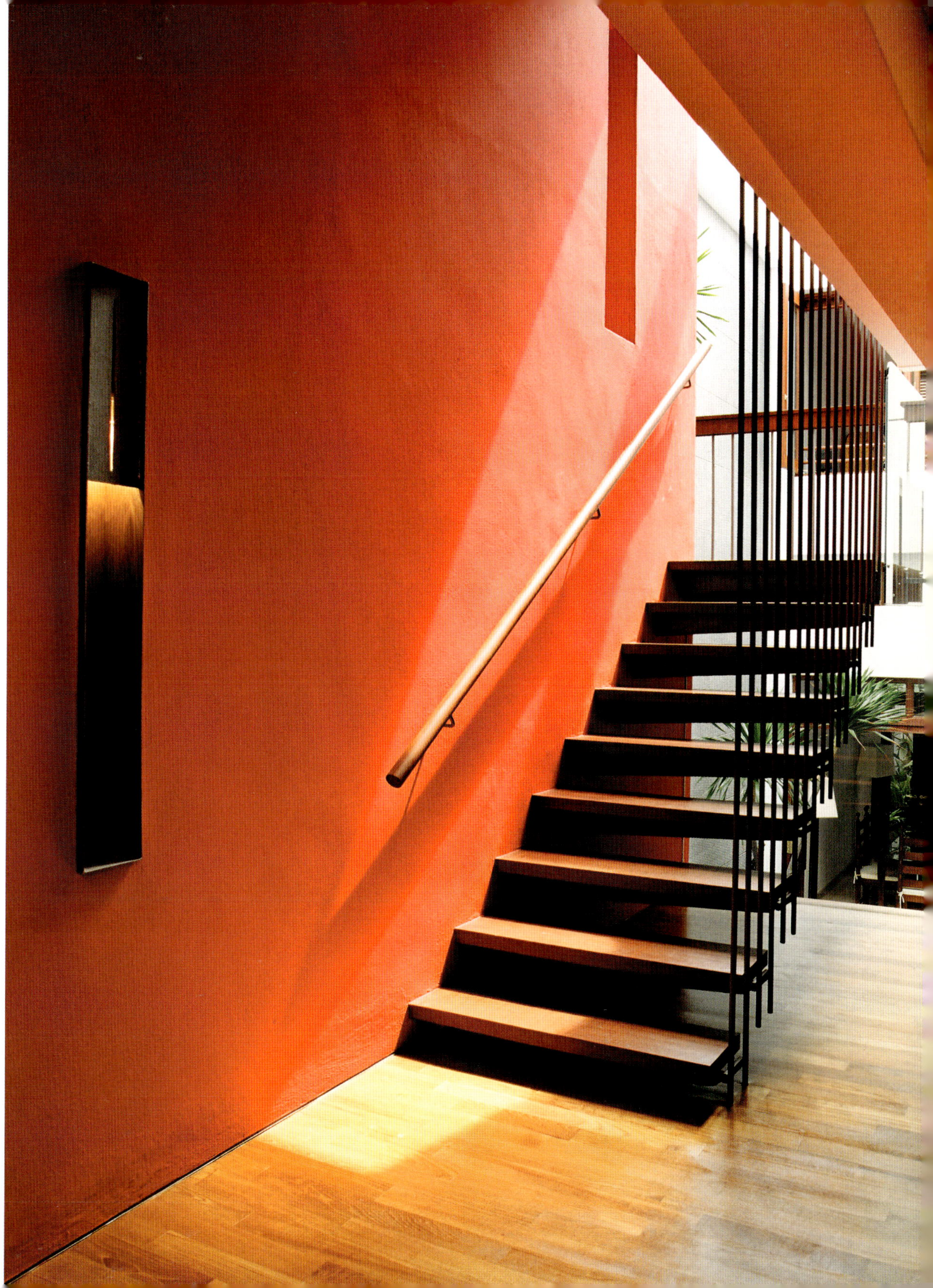

previous page, left to right the fish pond and greenery in the courtyard provide a contrast to the granite feature wall and soften the space; new staircase in the extension of the house is visually anchored by the central red wall. *above* new rear extension is set away from party wall so that more light enters the internal spaces. *opposite page, right* looking across the courtyard to the conserved front section of house. *far right* the roof terrace is sheltered by a canopy of large trees.

040 | Timeless Tropical

Conservation Townhouse at Cairnhill Road | 041

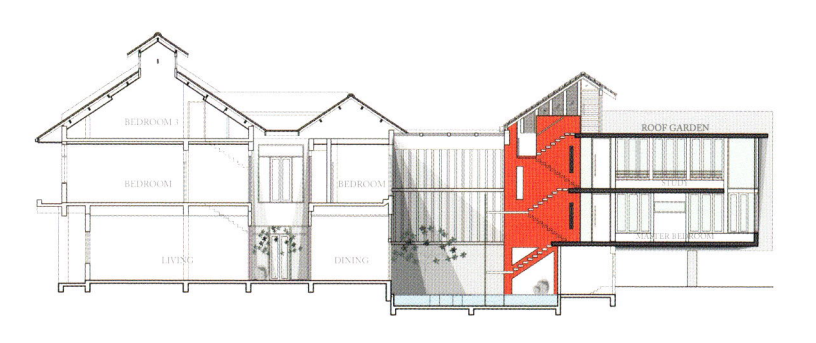

042 | Timeless Tropical

opposite page, clockwise from left double volume sitting area in the new extension has full height glass panels look out onto mature trees; bedroom opens into courtyard; master bathroom with filtered light from adjacent courtyard. *above* courtyard with retractable skylight above. *right* depth of house is punctuated by light from the two courtyards.

Conservation Townhouse at Cairnhill Road | 043

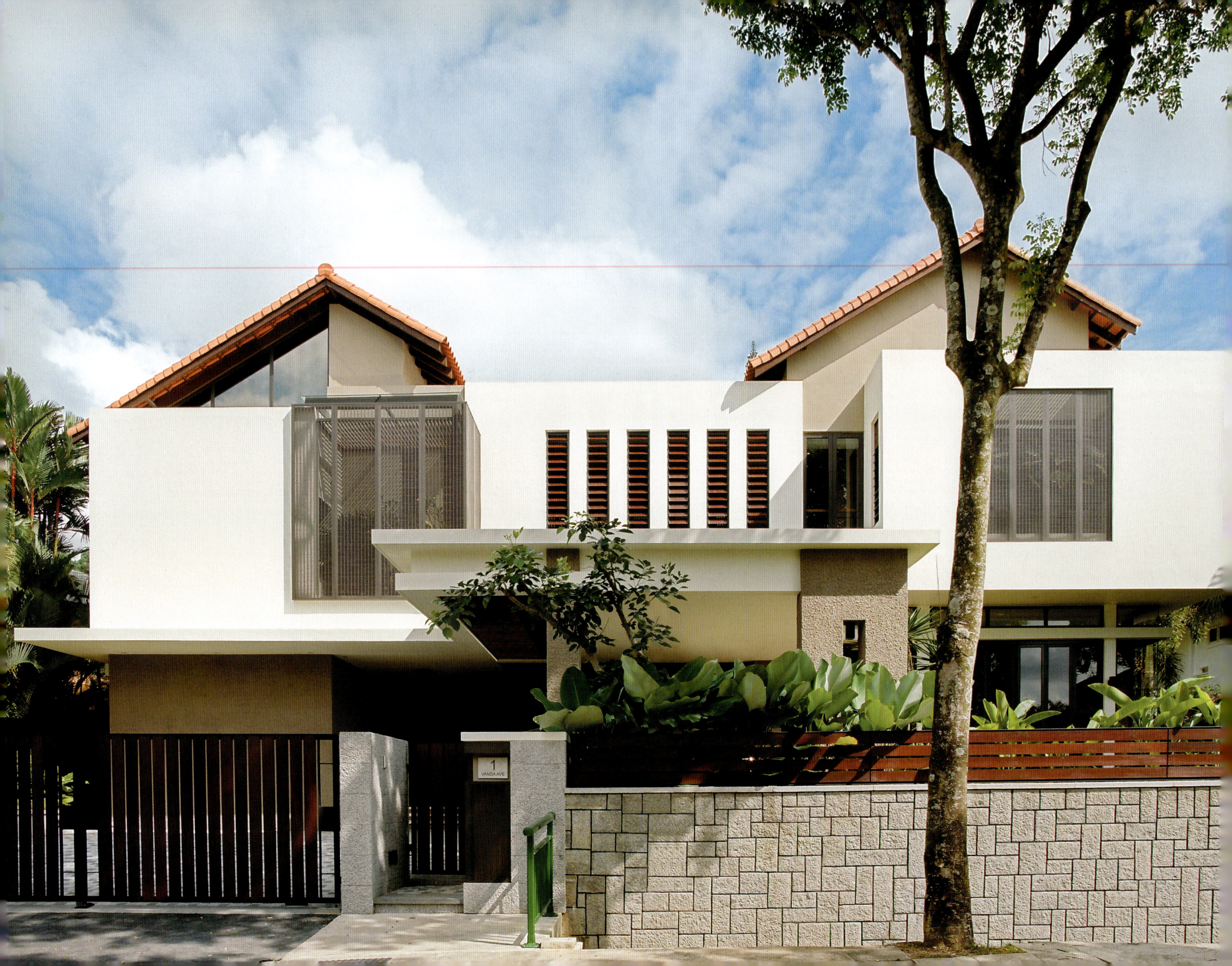
1
VANDA AVE

Detached House at Vanda Avenue

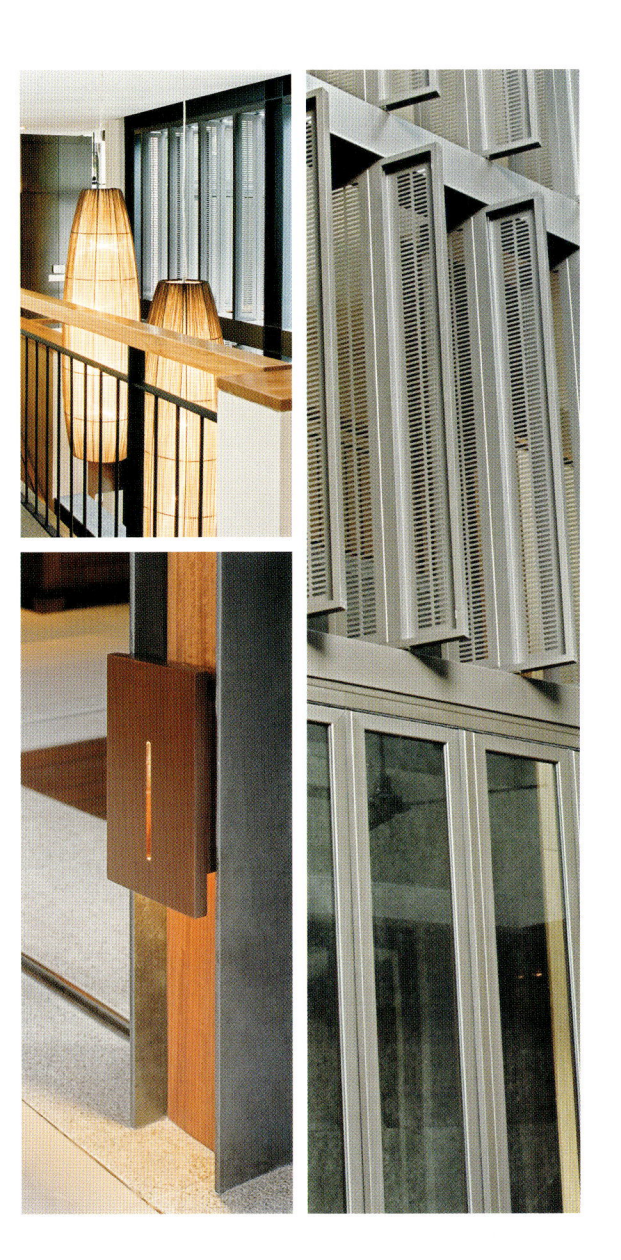

The plan of this house revolves around a covered courtyard space which opens on one side onto the garden. The living and dining rooms on the first storey and the family and master bedrooms on the upper storey all have full height windows opening onto the courtyard; creating a seamless spatial flow and making the courtyard truly the focus of family activity.

The main circulation core of the house similarly opens onto this central courtyard. Contained within a double volume space, the staircase and corridor connects the master wing to the rest of the house. Separating this core and the courtyard is a porous wall constructed out of mechanically pivoting perforated aluminium screens which make the interior of the house a totally naturally ventilated tropical living space.

Just as the interior flows seamlessly into the outdoors, the garden appears to continue beyond its space with the scenic landscaping of a large neighbouring house at its rear, hence creating the illusion of a much more expansive ground.

second storey   *first storey*

previous page front elevation, seen from vanda avenue. the two main wings (with tiled roofs) are linked by the corridor with strip louvred windows. *floor plans* the corridor link between the two wings also houses the central circulation space where the staircase is. one wing comprises the living room on the first storey and the master bedroom suite on the upper, while the other wing houses the remaining spaces of the house. all of these components are grouped around a central family area which is the covered outdoor patio. *left* close-up view of the link corridor between the two wings. louvred windows let in filtered light, provide natural ventilation and still maintain privacy for the occupants. *above* an outer "secondary" wall creates an intermediate zone for planting within the master bathroom. *opposite page, right and far right* the living room and master bedroom suite above opens up fully to the garden behind, so that the internal space flows out visually as well as physically.

046 | Timeless Tropical

Detached House at Vanda Avenue | 047

above three interior views of the link between the two wings. *right top and bottom* the central patio is a double volume space so that rooms on both floors can look in and connect with this outdoor family area. weather protection is provided by a glass and timber trellis roof. *opposite page, right* this central family patio is separated from the internal corridor and staircase by glass and aluminium folding doors and pivoting perforated aluminium screens above. the pivoting screens are mechanically operated with a remote control. when opened, the internal and external spaces merge as one. *far right* the corridor space is accentuated by shadow and sunlight coming through the screen.

048 | Timeless Tropical

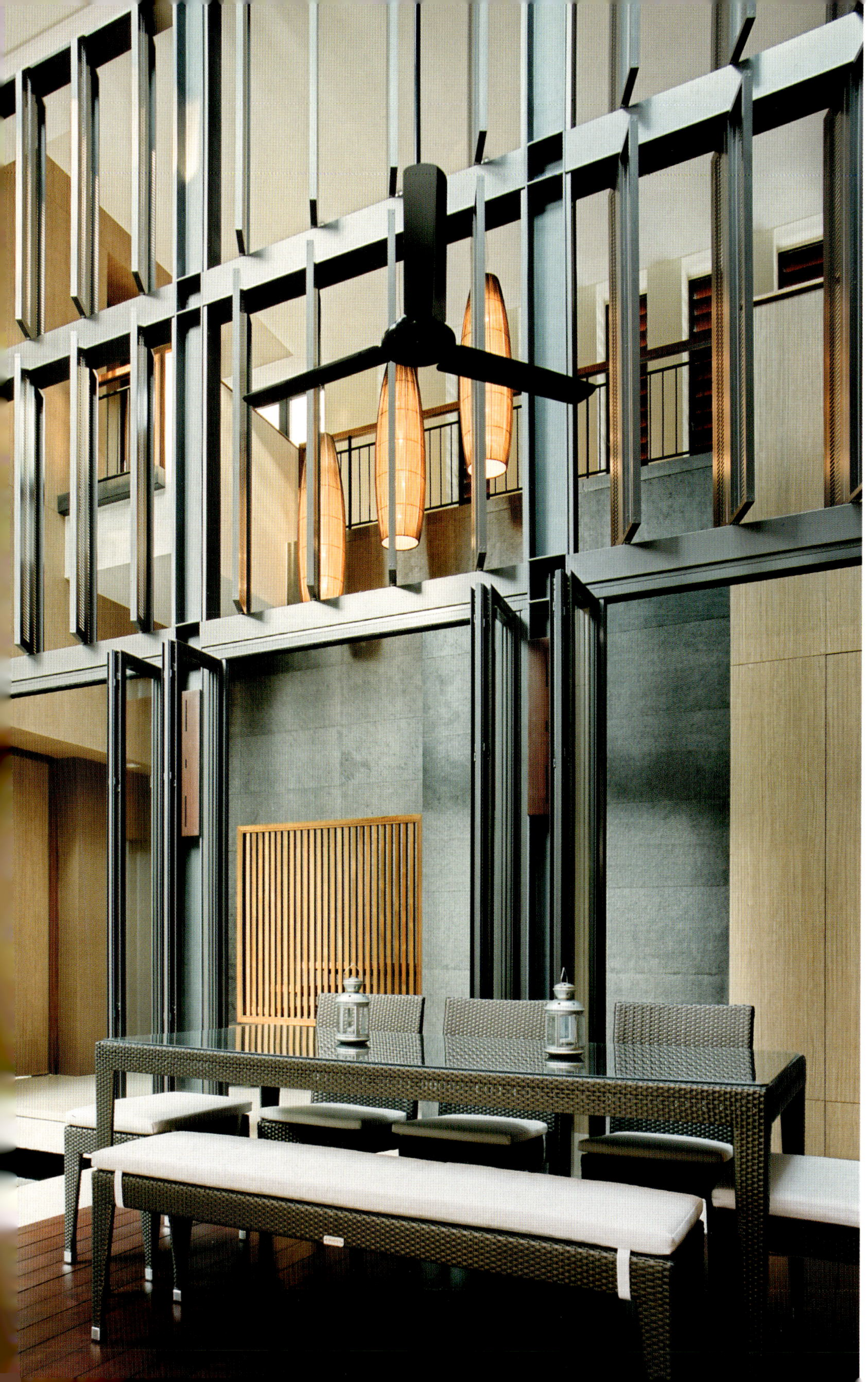
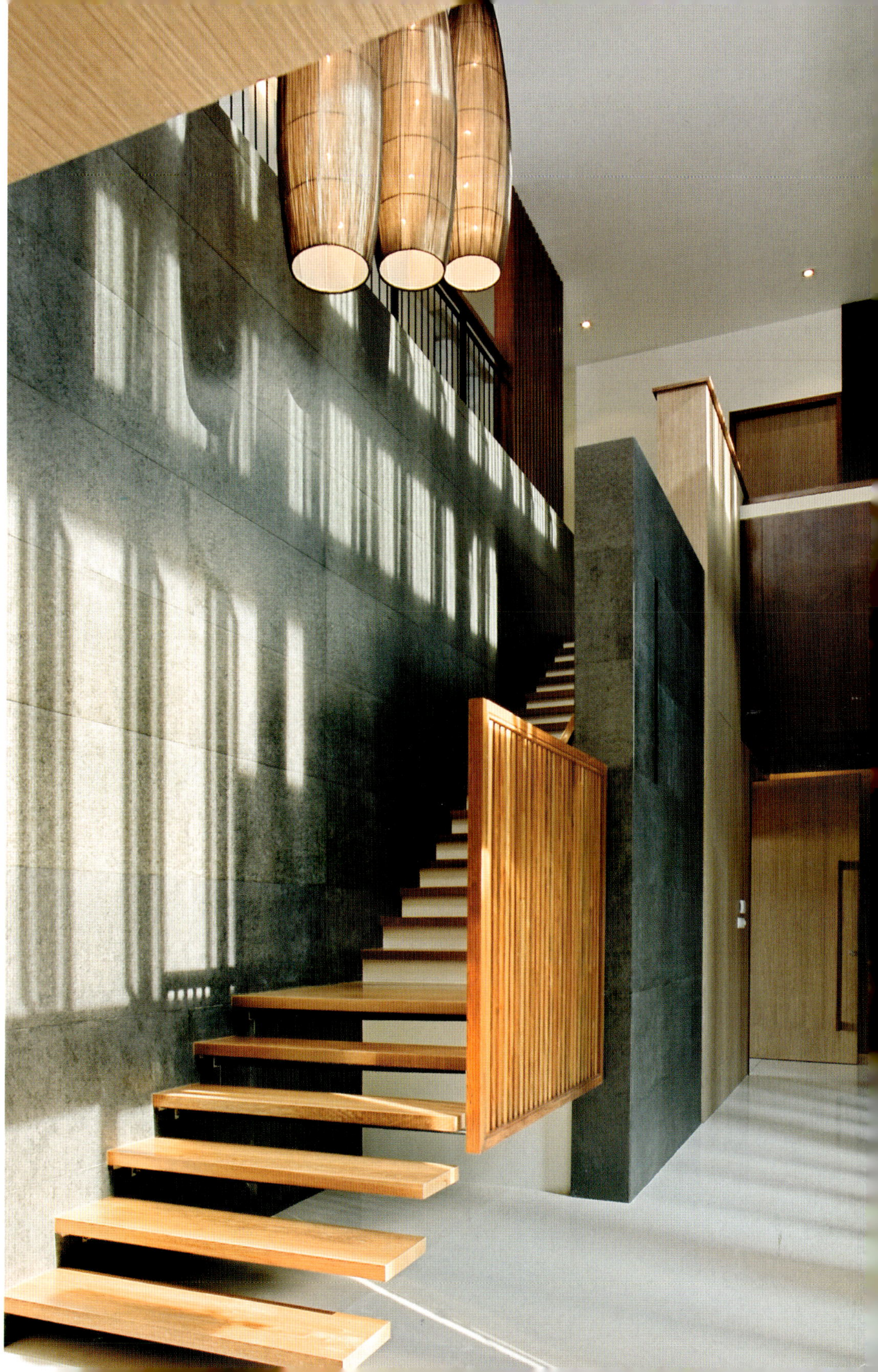

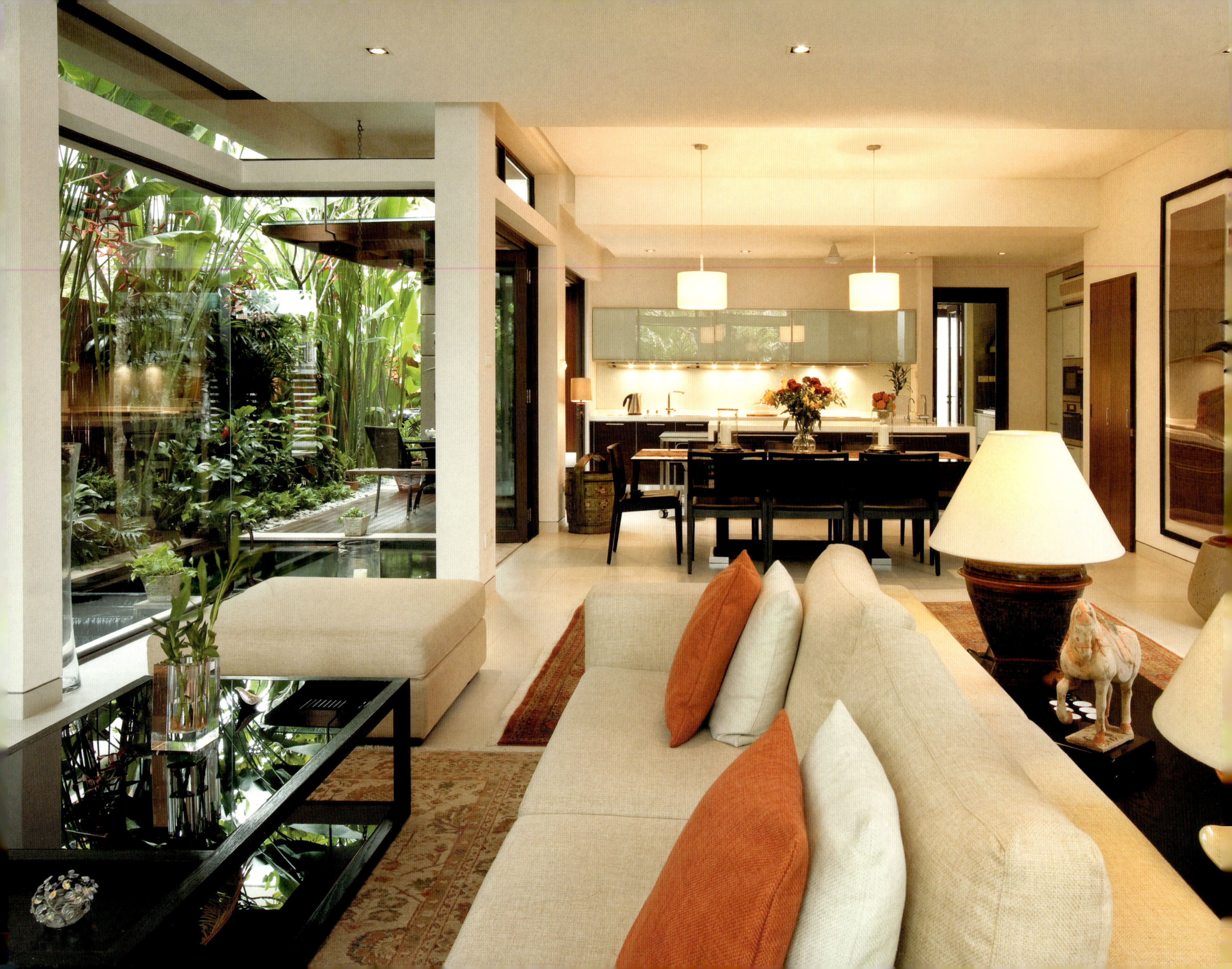

Semi-detached House at Meyer Road

This project encapsulates Timur's approach of designing a site, as opposed to just designing a house. The client's requirements for this project was extensive for a site with limits. Situated on a busy residential street with a large development across the street, the house has a quiet façade with lush landscaping to create adequate privacy for the living spaces within. Upon entering the house, the spaces for living, dining and cooking merges and extends into the garden. The line beyond the interior and exterior blurs as walls disappear when doors fold away to bring the multi-layered landscape to the doorstep. Although the garden is narrow and tight, the carefully chosen plants thrive and provide a soft respite from the hard surfaces of the adjacent estate. An intimate timber breakfast patio overlooks a fishpond with a luxuriant display of plants covering the bamboo fence at the side boundary.

A linear staircase brings one up to the bedrooms on the second storey and thereafter to the master suite at the attic level. The staircase is bathed in natural light that streams in from window openings at the roof. The master bedroom and bathroom are bathed in light as the roof soars above glass paneled walls. An aluminium-slatted screen provides sun and glare screen to the interior. A Ficus tree rises from a planter in the bathroom and literally brings the garden indoors. The master bedroom opens onto a roof terrace which is partially shaded by a large eave overhang and its hard surfaces are softened by luxuriant green foliage on the terrace and rippling sounds from a small water feature.

previous glazing and doors that open completely integrate the outside and interior spaces; lush landscaping screen the house from the outside. *left* the outdoor room is enhanced by landscaping and water features. *above* the removal of boundaries between living, dining and cooking areas liberates the space. *opposite page, left to right* light filters down from the attic windows and cast shadow patterns in the stairwell; privacy is provided to the master bathroom by plants and aluminium slatted screen.

052 | Timeless Tropical

attic storey *second storey* *first storey*

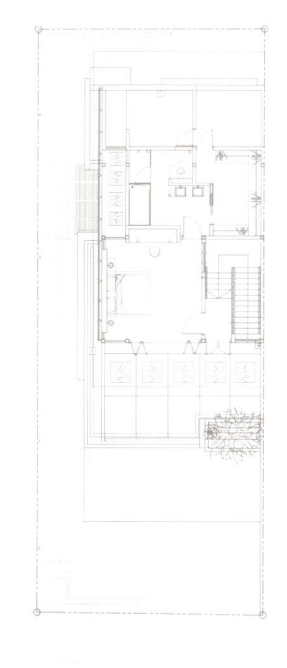

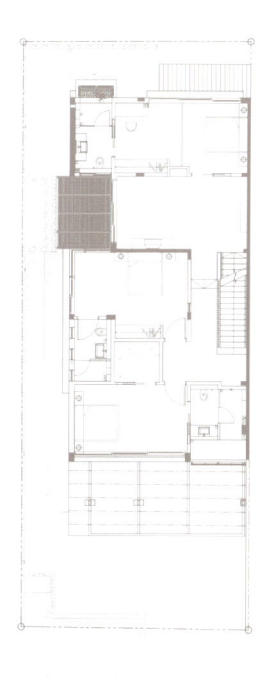

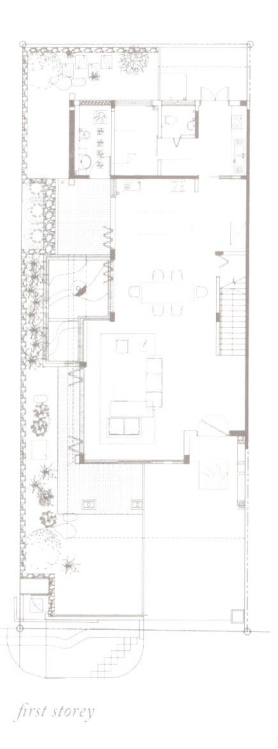

Semi-detached House at Meyer Road | 053

Terrace House at Makepeace Road

This corner terrace house was built in 1924 and features an original two-storey front section as well as a three-storey new extension at its rear. As with all houses done by Timur Designs, it is based on the concept that a house is not a just a box of rooms, but rather, a progression of spaces. Thus, behind the traditional façade, there is the openness of the living spaces juxtaposed with the use of water, landscape and the clever play of natural light to create a delightful ambience for tropical living.

Pre-war houses typically have structural timber floor joists that span the width of the house between two load-bearing brick walls. This structural integrity has been maintained despite having the soaring volume within the original roof form opened up with living spaces on the different floors. These spaces focus around this central volume through which the open staircase rises.

Besides maintaining the historical façade and respecting the original streetscape, Timur has also not compromised on the fact that the wet areas in such pre-war houses were always built at the rear so that the timber flooring in the main house would not affected by dampness. Adhering to this consideration, Timur erected the new bathroom wing to abut the (length) side of the house instead.

The rear section of the house has three floors with the height kept discreet so that it does not overwhelm the original roof of the house. To avoid mimicking the idioms of the original main house, this rear section was deliberately lightened up through the use of a light-weight metal roof and a screen of adjustable aluminium louvres on the side wall that opens onto the garden. The screen has a privacy function while providing a homogenous front to the various internal activities. The site is a triangular one which splays out at the rear. This feature allows a series of surprises as one walks through the house. The progression brings one through the living space, then to the open kitchen and dining spaces which are the main focal areas. The dining space is designed as a pavilion surrounded by greenery. It uses timber and steel to carry the lightest of enclosures. But what is especially significant is that the solid boundary wall at the rear has been removed so that the dining pavilion enjoys a direct visual connection to the public park immediately behind it through transparent glass screens.

Water is a prominent feature of the house with the use of a two-tier pond that wraps around the living space and a play pool which comes up to the kitchen and dining deck. The play of sunlight on water and the sound of water trickling in the pond results in a visual and auditory delight that masks this house's city centre location.

The finishes within the house employ a combination of textures and colours to enhance the modern setting with the intensity of the Asian palette. The richness of details offset the dynamism of ever changing natural light, thus presenting different visual perspectives and delight to the occupants daily.

054 | Timeless Tropical

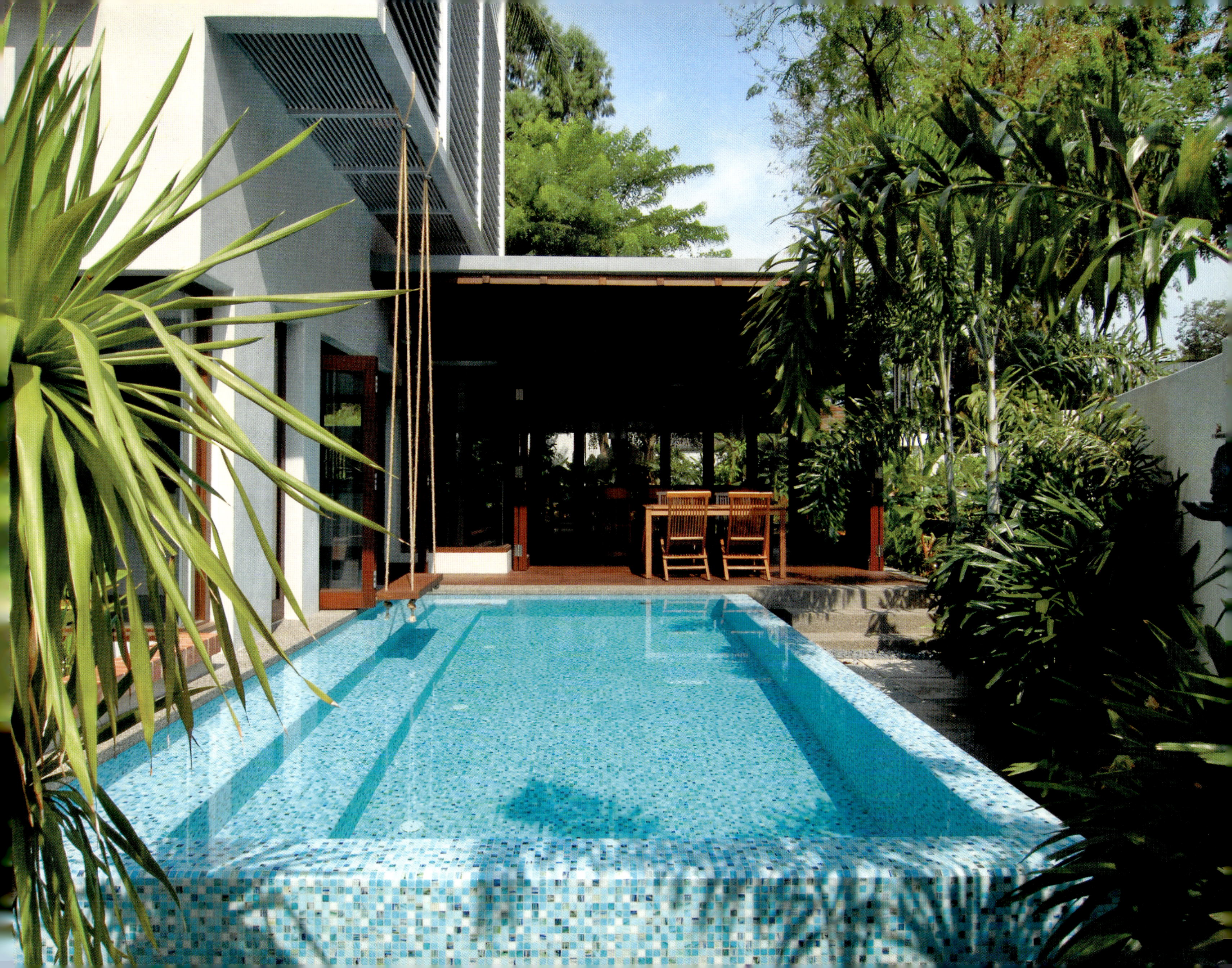

056 | Timeless Tropical

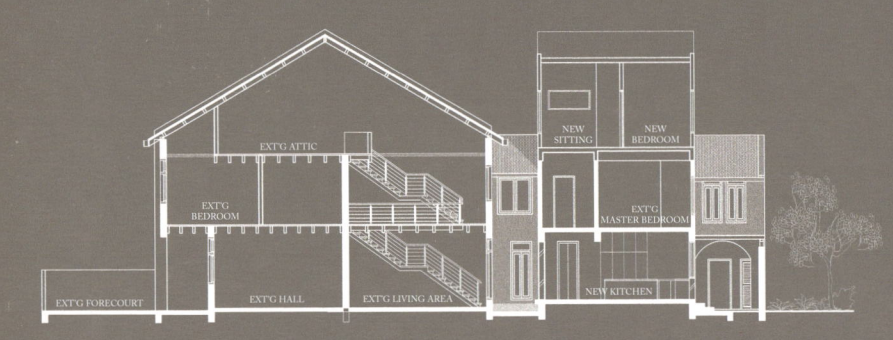

previous page view across garden to the dining area and the public park behind; the sparkling glass mosaics provide a contrast to the rich timbers and greenery of the surroundings. *opposite page, far left* original front façade is retained to keep the character of the original house. *left* electronically-controlled louvres provide privacy to the internal rooms in the new rear extension. *this page* different water elements in the house.

Terrace House at Makepeace Road | 057

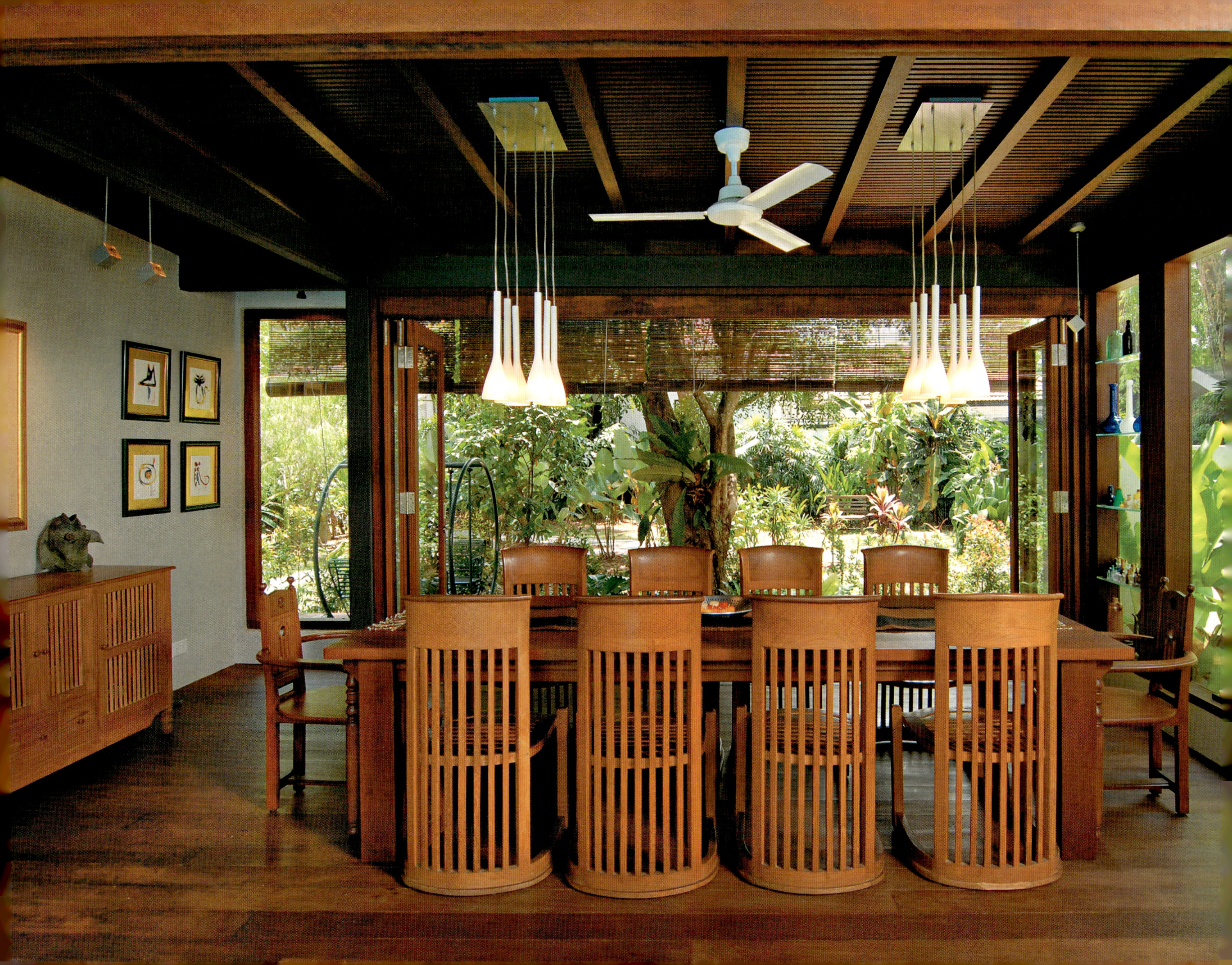

opposite page the dining pavilion is surrounded by lush greenery. sliding and folding doors open the space to the garden facing the park. *above* from the side of the pool, similar doors also extend the dining space outwards.

Terrace House at Makepeace Road

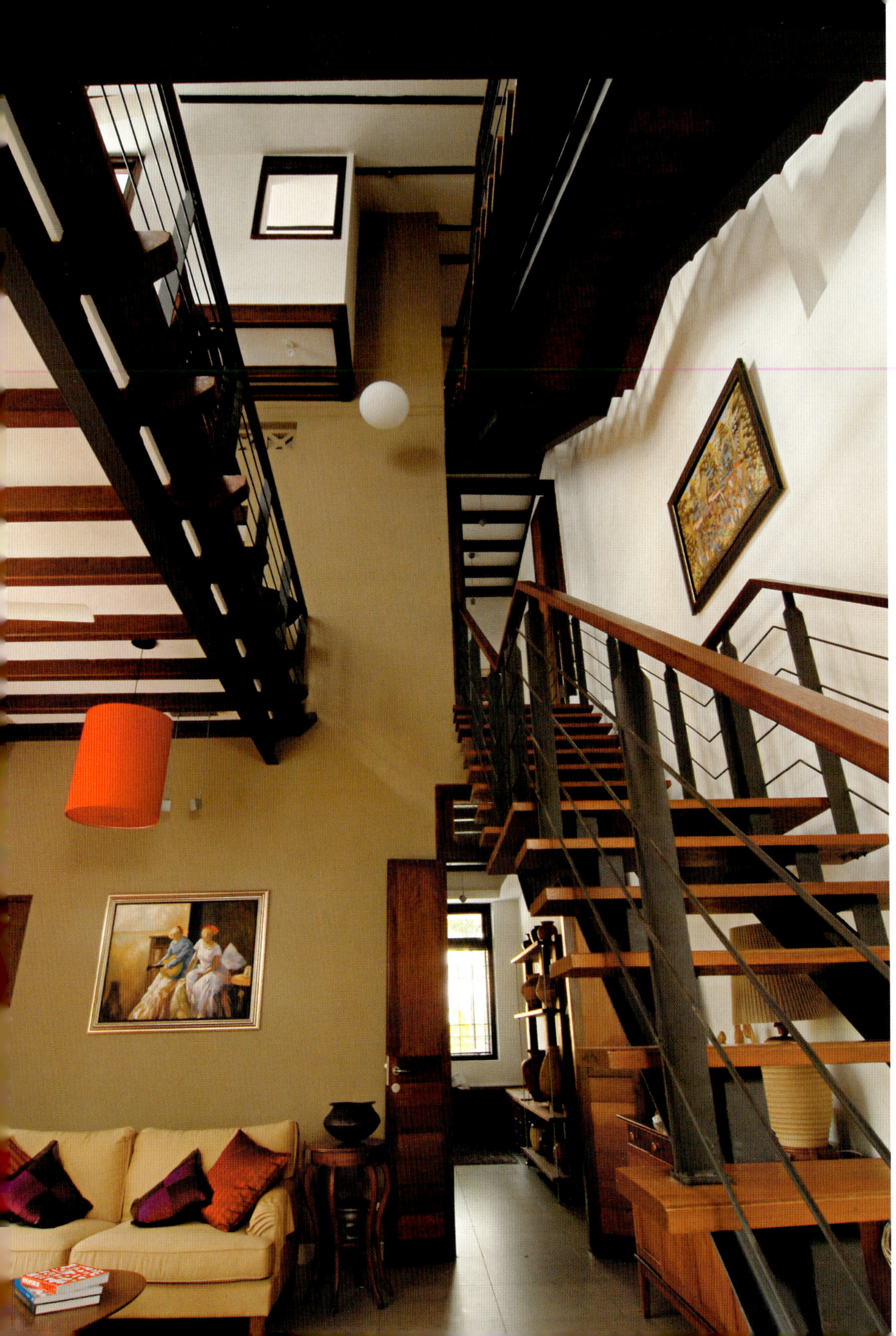

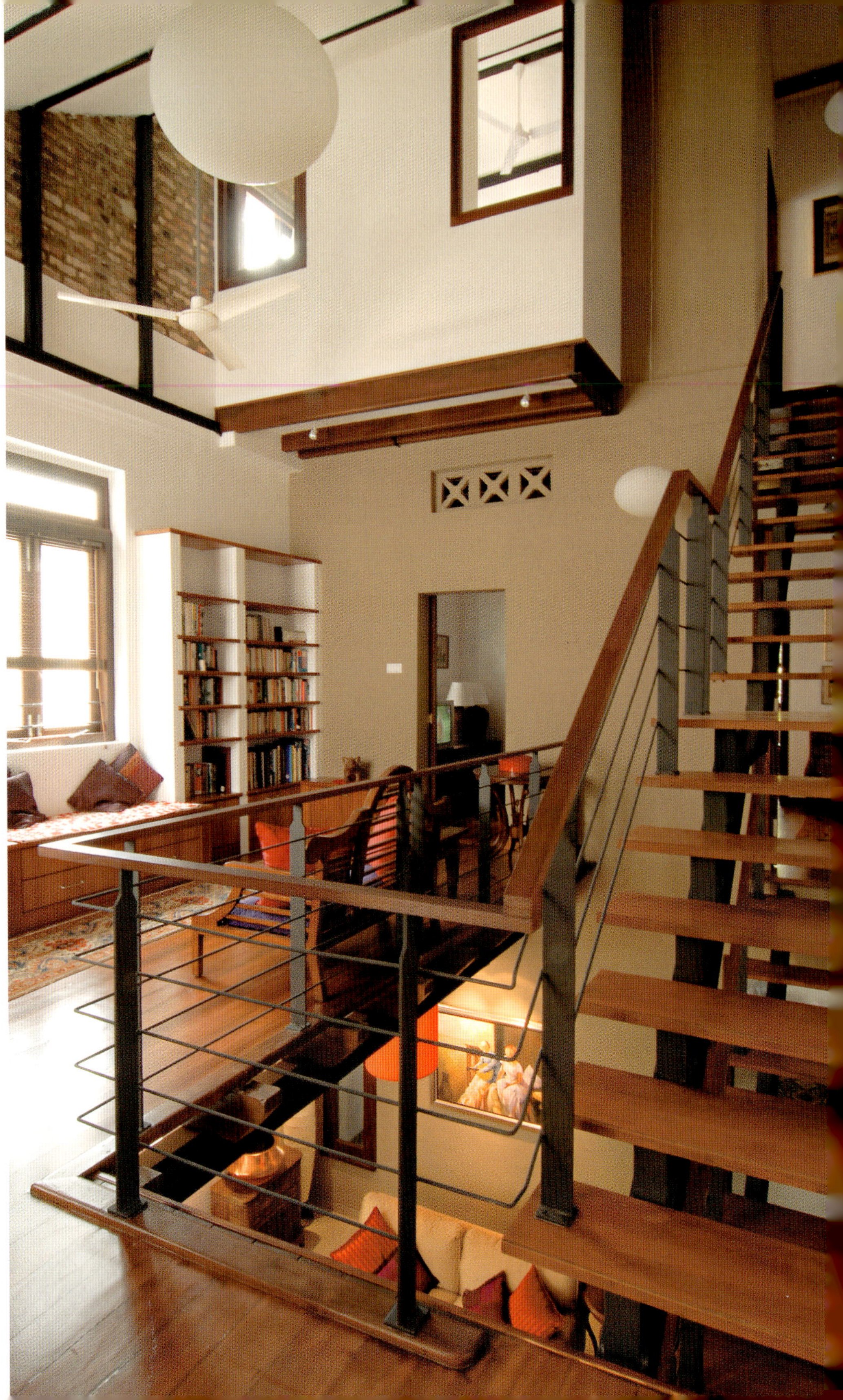

opposite page, far left the spatial volume in the original house is opened up and visually linked from level to level. *left* an attic is created in the original roof space. *top* the rich tones of the furnishings enhance the deep hues of the timber. *bottom* looking down the third level volume from the attic. *right* open library area on the second level provides connectivity from the front section to the rear of the house.

Terrace House at Makepeace Road | 061

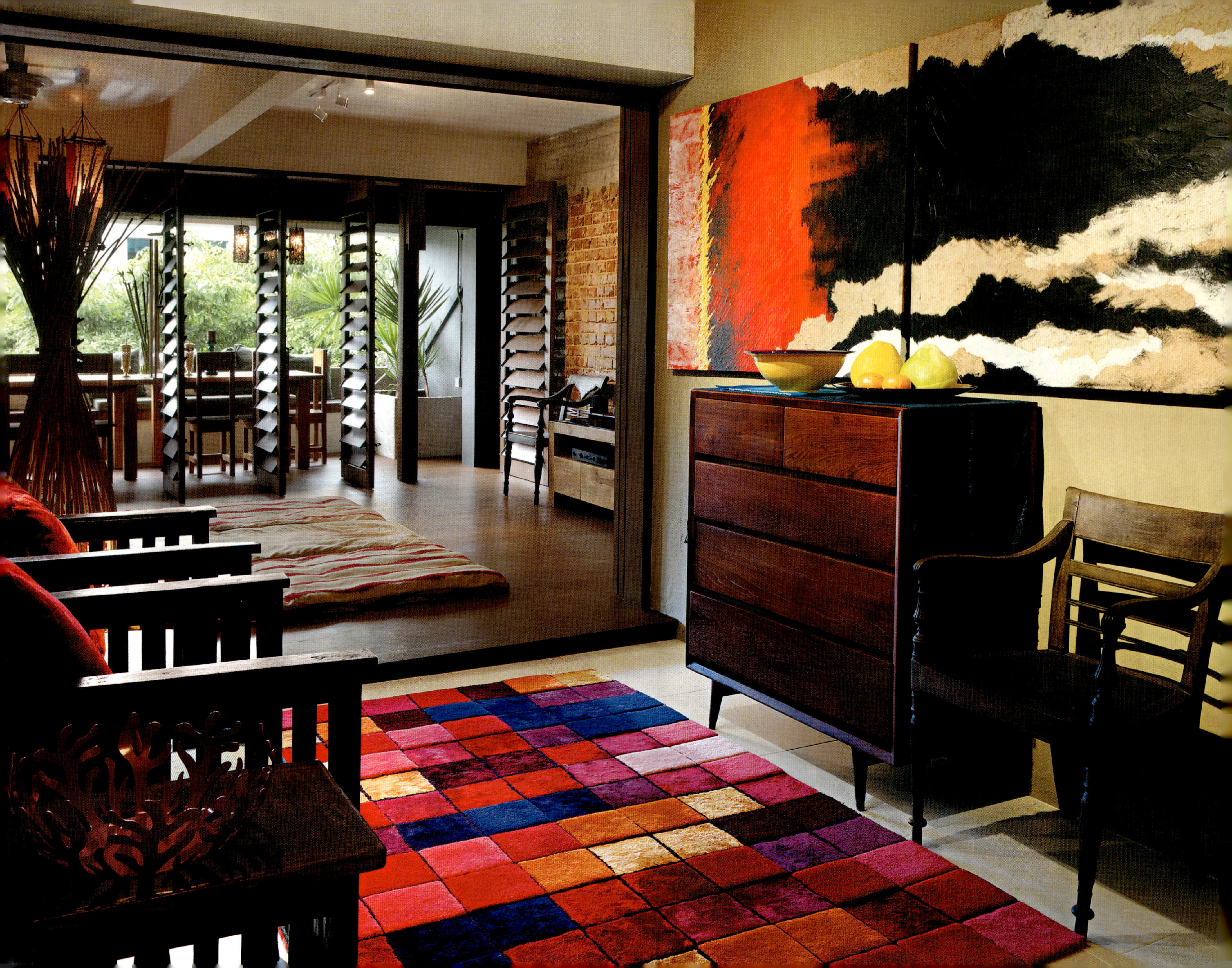

Apartment at Chay Yan Street, Tiong Bahru

The walk-up apartments in Tiong Bahru were the first multi-storey public housing units to be built in Singapore in the late 1950s.

Modeled after the traditional shophouse form and complete with air-wells and open-air rear courtyards, these flats undoubtedly retain the scale of the old streetscape. Covered walkways and off-street parking give this housing estate a unique character which is becoming a rarity in Singapore.

At 900 square feet, the apartments in their original state can appear dark and claustrophobic. However, once the partition walls have been demolished, the newly enlarged space is more airy and bathed in daylight – the quintessential way tropical living is intended to be.

Within a gutted-out old shell, a completely new space is created. The solid walls separating the rooms and the balcony in the original flat have been replaced with pivoting timber louvred screens which when fully open, connect the living space to the outdoors.

Wall plaster has been hacked off from one of the walls to reveal the brick-laying craft of the old days, a handiwork which is sadly largely missing today.

previous page with the original brick walls removed, all the rooms merge into one space, opening out onto the balcony and the outdoors. sliding glass panels and pivoting louvred panels have the option to be closed to partition up the spaces when needed. *left t*he main living area is separated from the balcony by the pivoting timber louvred screens. *opposite page, right* plaster removed from the existing wall to reveal old brickwork from yesteryear. *far right* the existing balcony was widened to create a semi-outdoor dining room.

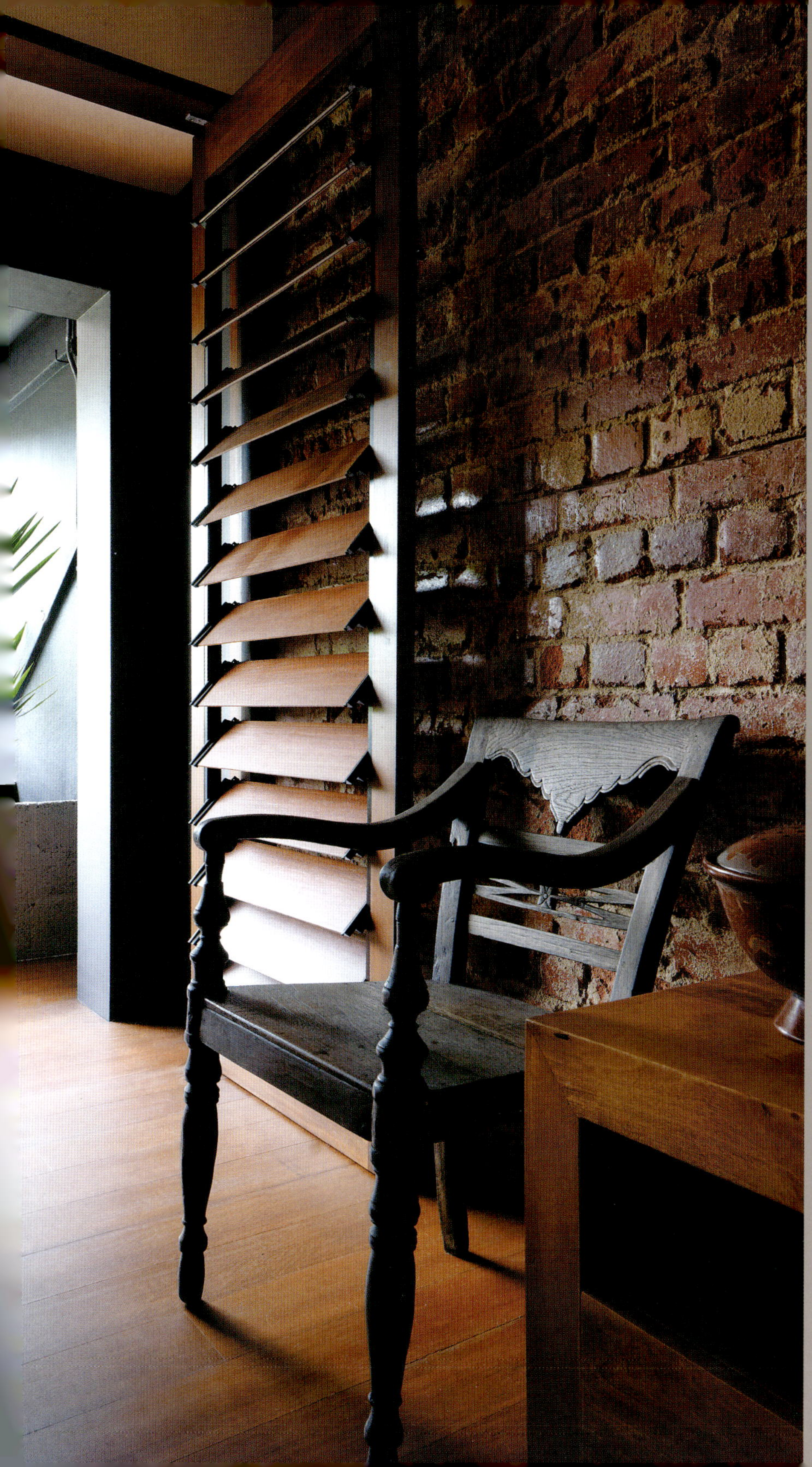

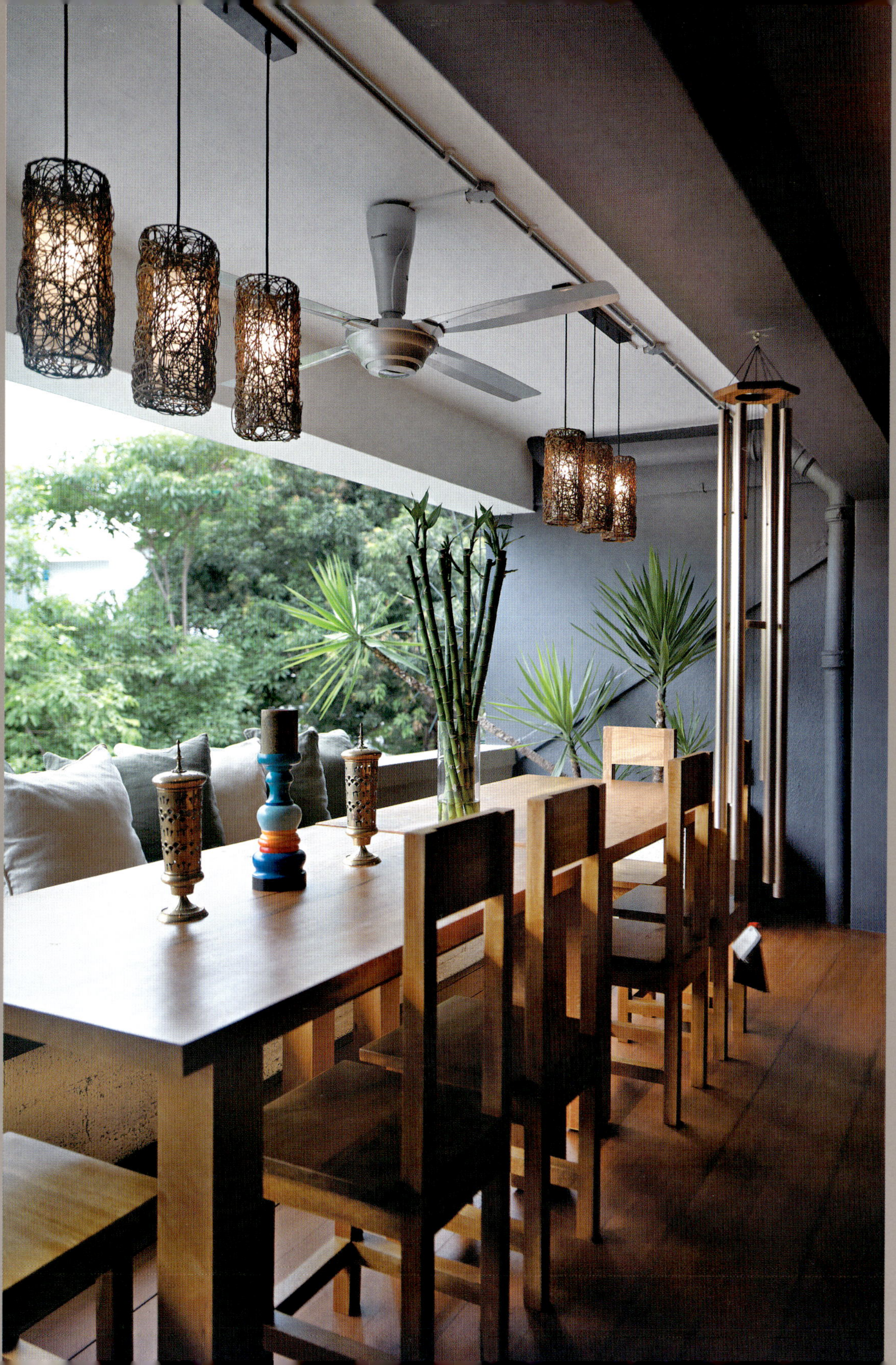

066 | Timeless Tropical

opposite page and right demonstrating the flexibility and adaptability of the pivoting timber louvred screens. they may be fully closed for privacy or to air-condition the living room, partially open to control the amount of natural light and ventilation, or fully open to fully connect the interior space with the outdoors.

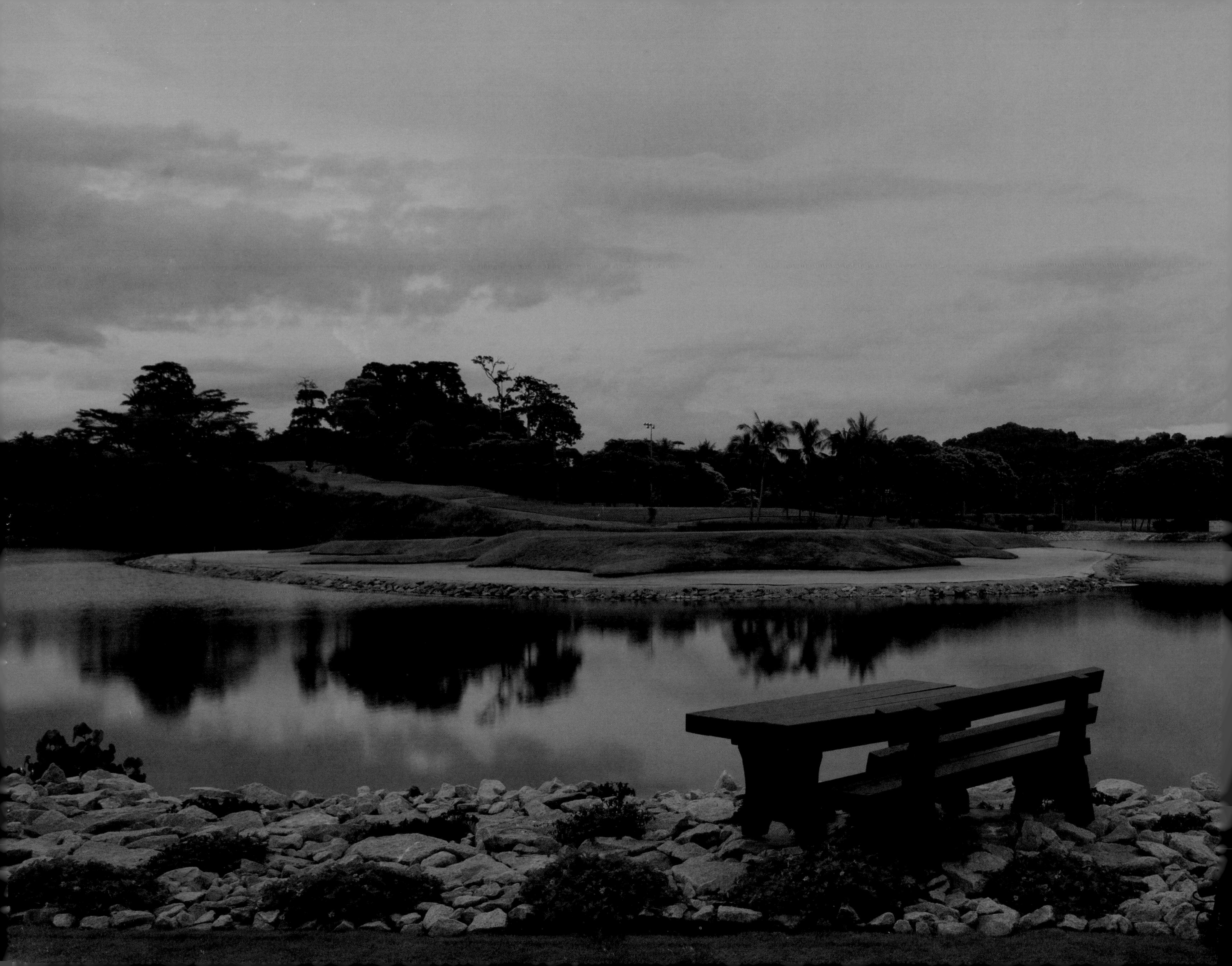

Waterfront Living

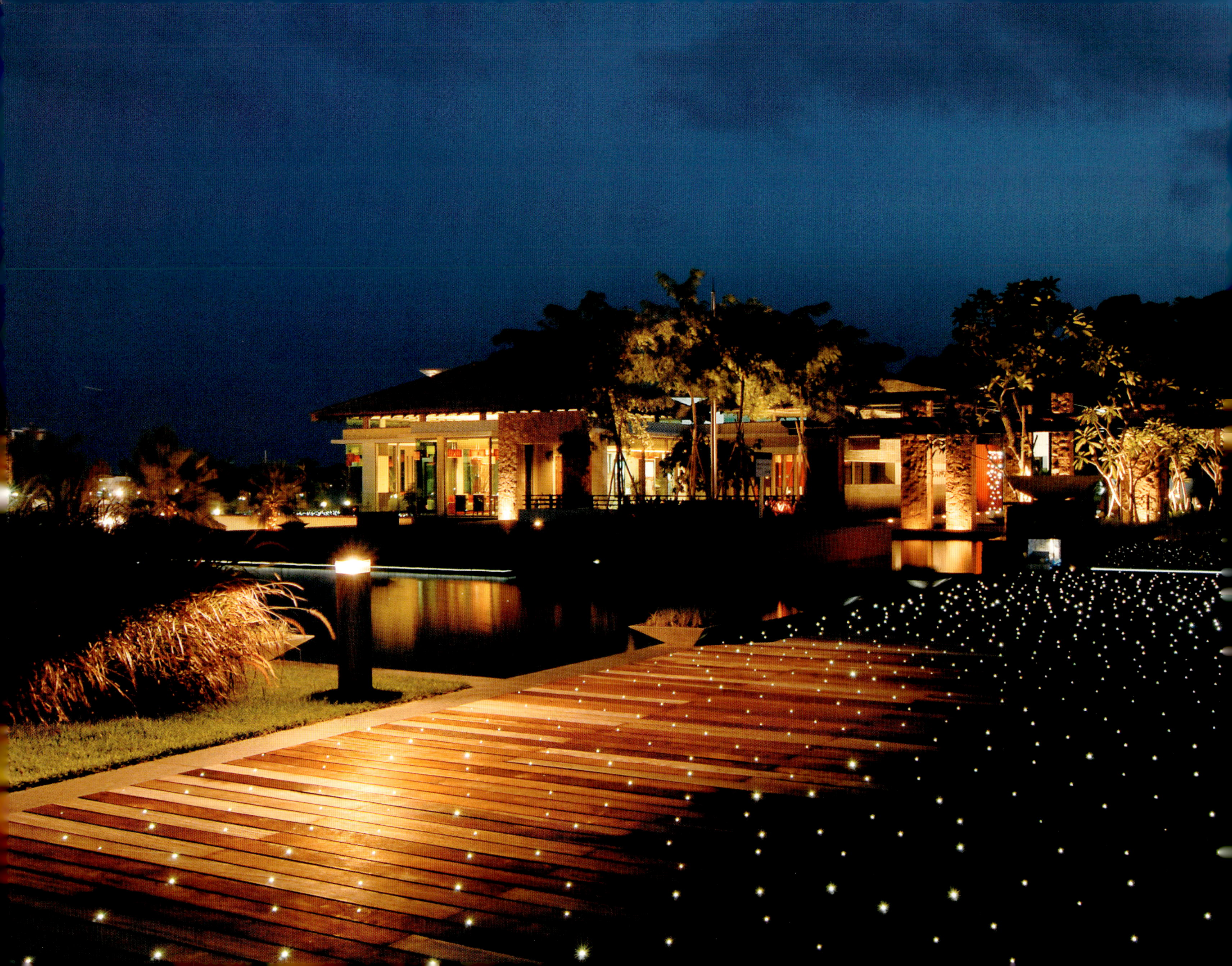

Arrival Plaza, Sentosa Cove

The Arrival Plaza is conceived as a park to greet residents and visitors upon entering the exclusive waterfront housing enclave of Sentosa Cove. With such scenic surroundings, it is essential to maintain an unobstructed visual axis to the marina as one enters Sentosa Cove. This is achieved by virtue of the difference in level between the promenade and the access road, allowing two levels of car-parking to be sunken below the plaza.

To reduce the hefty impact of a three-storey building housing some 900 car-park lots, the building is split into three linked blocks, with landscaped spines in between the carpark blocks. These spines weave through landscaped foliage to lead pedestrians down to the waterfront promenade.

For clarity, a simple structural system of flat slab and tapering columns with circular drop-panels is adopted and the inspired visage resembles a forest of concrete trees.

On the plaza level, the Sentosa Cove land sales office has incorporated elements of waterfront housing including reflecting pools, timber decks and trellises, stone-clad walls and lush landscaping. The whole intention of such a space is to help potential buyers envision what a home in Sentosa Cove might look like.

previous page at night, recessed fibre optic lights illuminate the timber decks. *left and middle* the covered linkway. *right* the glass lift connects the plaza at ground level to the carpark levels below. *opposite page* the arrival plaza, lushly landscaped with an unobstructed view to the marina. The carpark levels are tucked beneath, respecting the drop in the land profile.

072 | Timeless Tropical

Arrival Plaza, Sentosa Cove | 073

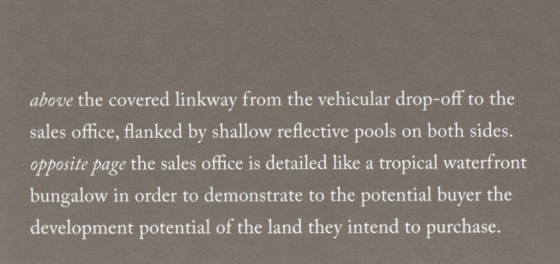

above the covered linkway from the vehicular drop-off to the sales office, flanked by shallow reflective pools on both sides. *opposite page* the sales office is detailed like a tropical waterfront bungalow in order to demonstrate to the potential buyer the development potential of the land they intend to purchase.

074 | Timeless Tropical

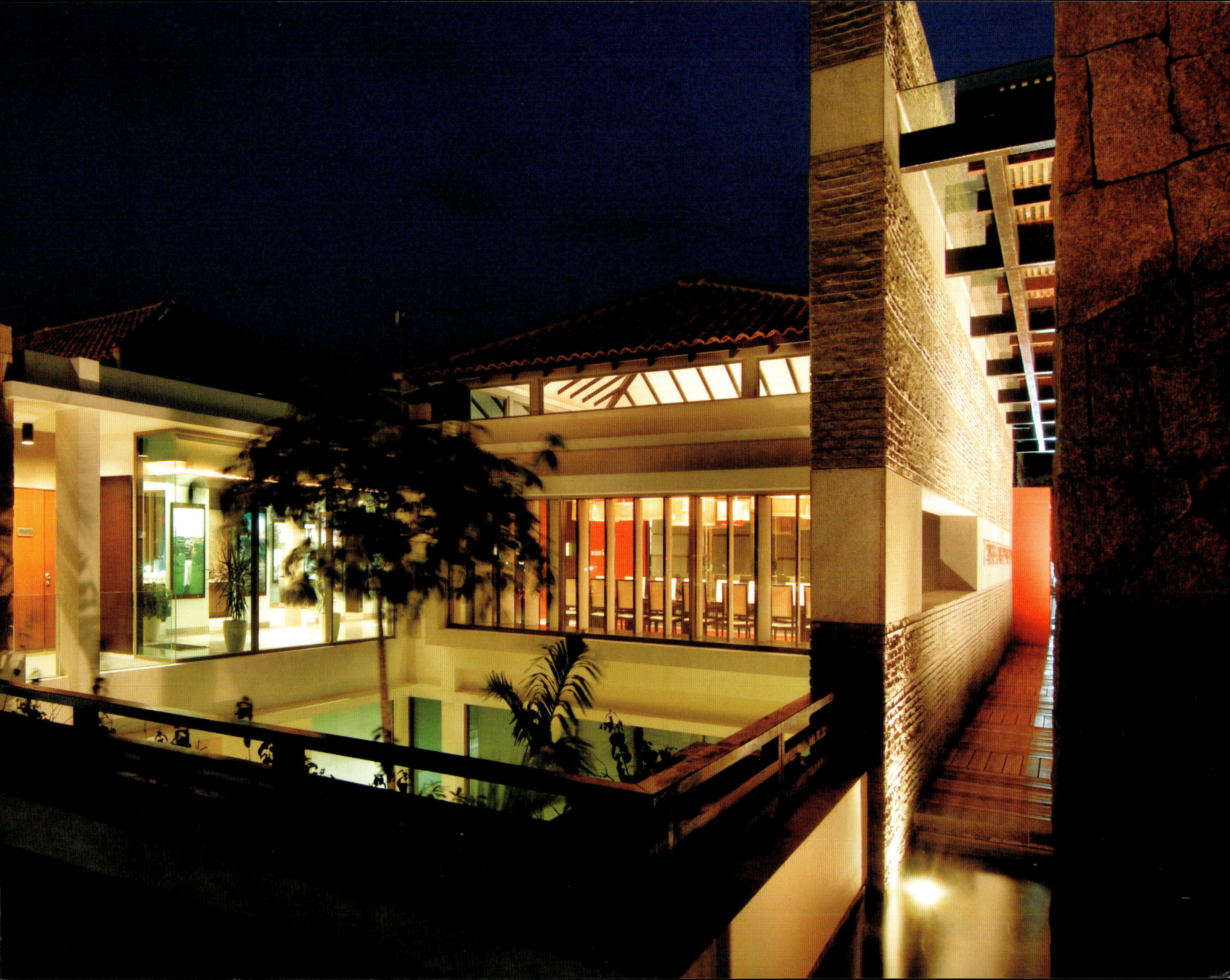

left the linkway leading towards the waterfront promenade and the marina. *opposite page, top and bottom row* courtyards, timber trellises and vertical planting help to conceal the concrete structure of the carpark, turning it into a lush, elegant plaza. *far right* the carpark structure is made up of tapering columns and circular drop panels resembling concrete trees. *section drawing* illustrates how the car-parking is tucked within the green, leaving just the plaza and the sales office above ground. the pedestrian is then led down the descending levels of the arrival plaza onto the waterfront promenade.

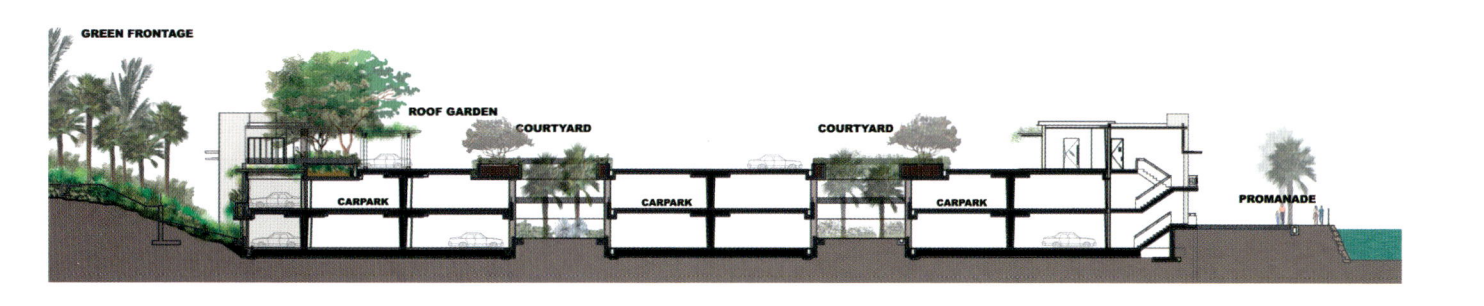

Arrival Plaza, Sentosa Cove | 077

left the interior of the sales office, with views out to the marina. *above* daylight streaming down the staircase that links the sales office to the office below. such details can be easily adapted to the design of bungalows in sentosa cove. *opposite page* the entrance to the sales office.

Arrival Plaza, Sentosa Cove | 079

Sentosa Cove House One

Situated on the seafront of Sentosa Cove, this resort-style house comprises the main house component and a smaller pool house.

The front of the house is deliberately designed with a 'closed' façade – a red granite rubble wall forming a barrier to the front door in order to maintain privacy. This is due to the fact that fences and gates are disallowed in this waterfront housing enclave.

Once inside the house, the space opens out physically as well as visually to the swimming pool and a landscaped pond, of which beyond is the sea.

The main house is configured like a cluster of pavilions, where the individual bedrooms, study and formal living room are expressed as independent volumes linked together by a central circulation space. Externally, this circulation space is roofed with a concrete slab in order to accentuate the pitched tiled roofs over the other spaces.

Glass and timber louvred windows are used extensively on the façade to make the walls porous for the influx of daylight and sea breeze, complementing the tropical lifestyle the house has been intended for. In the patio outside the living room, the double-height space achieves the same effect with the use of perforated aluminium sheets.

The basement floor of the main house is connected to the pool house via an external granite staircase and opens up fully into a reflecting pool of water, which is open to the sky to allow the basement floor to flow spatially outwards.

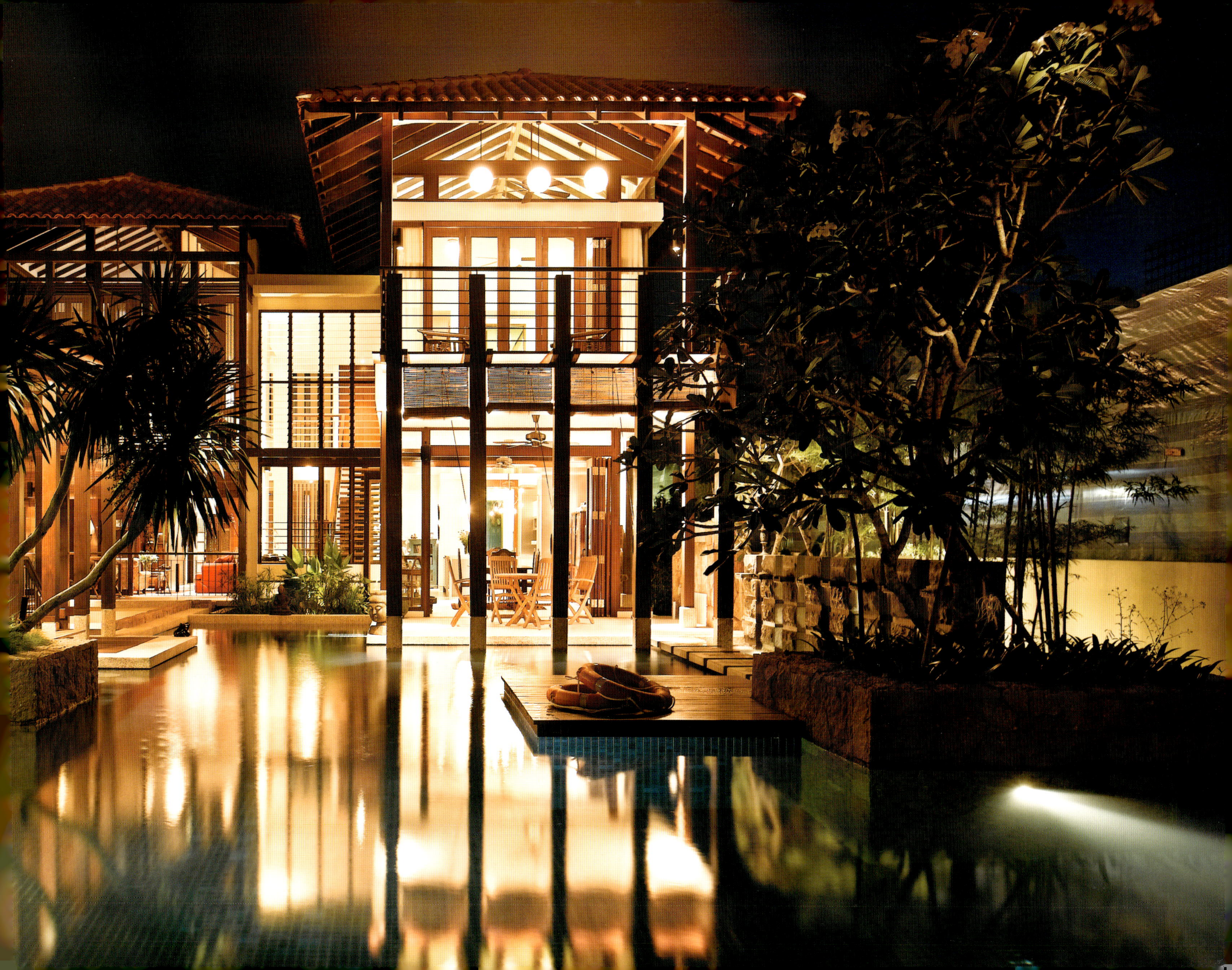

previous page night view of the side of the house that opens to the sea, epitomising the spirit of waterfront living in sentosa cove. *left* view of link to the pool house and the staircase down to the sunken courtyard and the basement family room. *right* the pool house and the swimming pool, with the sea in horizon. *opposite page* view from the house across the pond and the swimming pool, towards the sea. *opposite page, far right* island' in the pool connected to the main house by stepping stones with a series of stone-clad walls and water spouts on its left. *section drawing* illustrates the relationship between the basement family room, the sunken courtyard and the main house.

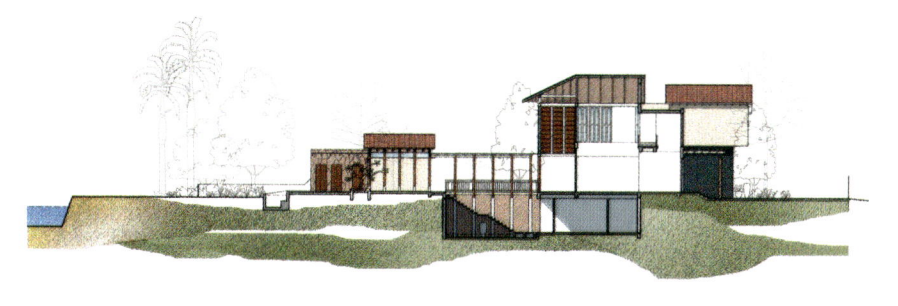

Sentosa Cove House One | 083

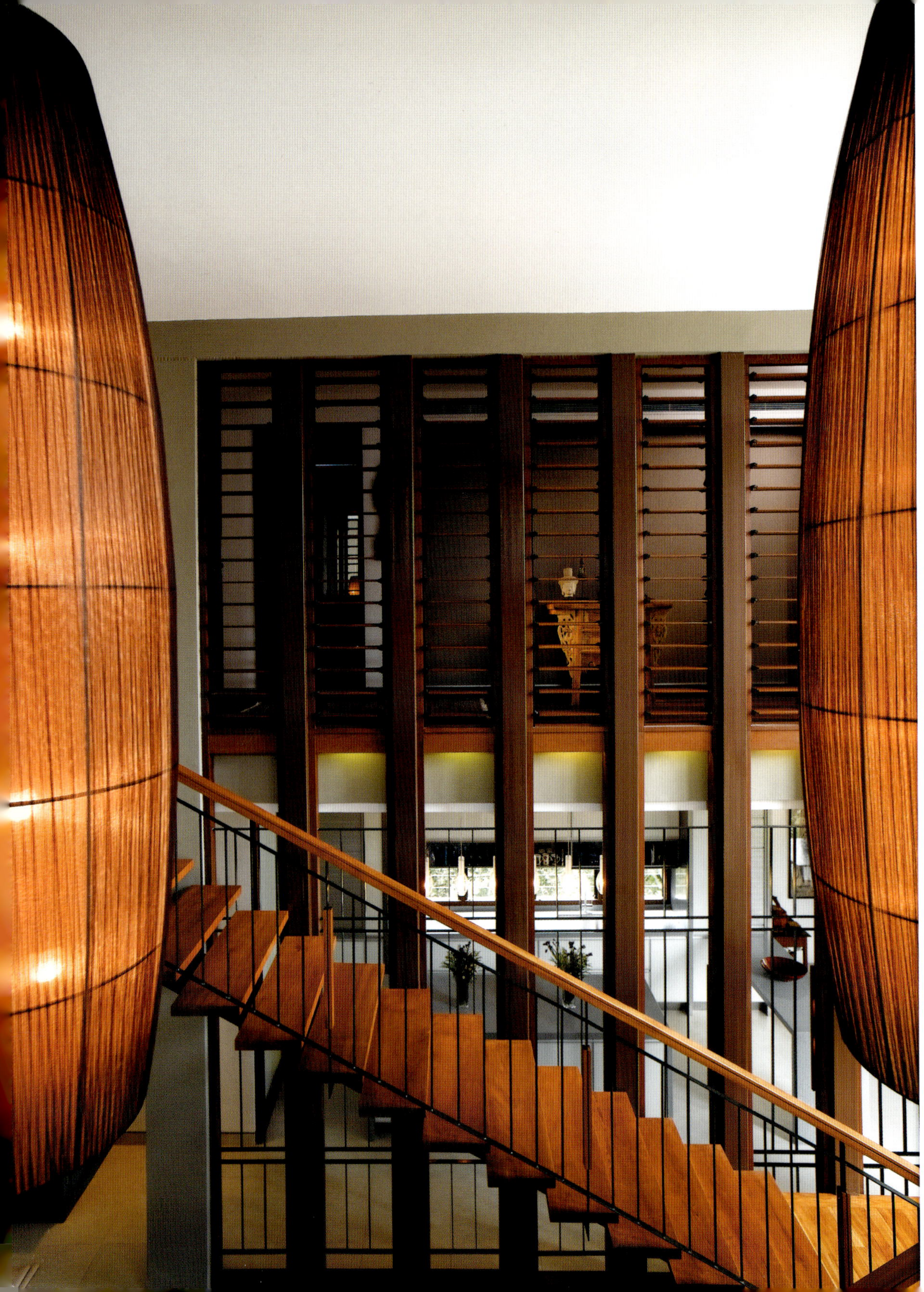
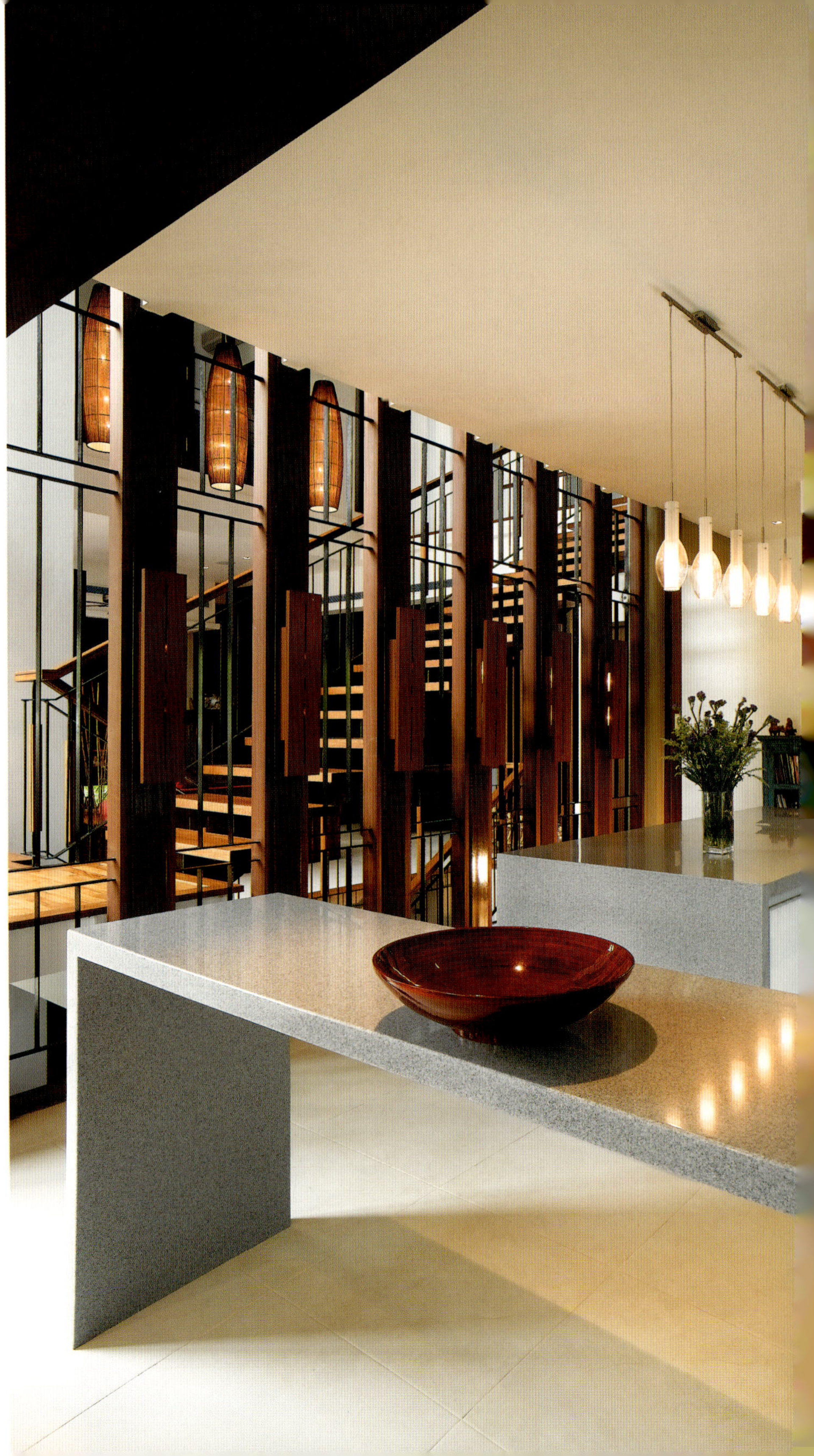

opposite page, far left and left timber louvred screens continue from the external façade into the house, forming screens separating the master bedroom above and the kitchen below from the double volume living room, and yet still providing visual continuity. *above* looking down into the double volume living room. *right* the internal staircase links to the basement.

Sentosa Cove House One | 085

086 | Timeless Tropical

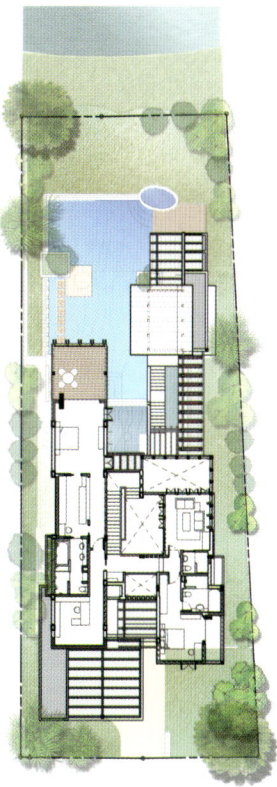

second storey   *first storey*

opposite page, clockwise from left the living room opens onto a patio which links to the pool house. screens and blinds provide protection from rain and sun; the master bedroom opening out onto a balcony with views of the sea; stepping stones over a pond linking the living room patio to the dining room; view of the staircase from the basement. *right* the sunken courtyard is also a reflective pool. the steps lead up to the pool house while the link bridge on the right connects the pool house to the living room, thus completing a circulation loop through the house.

Timeless Tropical

Sentosa Cove House Two

This house is built on one of the smallest plots for detached houses in the southern part of Sentosa Cove. However, across the waterway, is a golf course putting green which gives the house a much more spacious feel despite the size of the land that it sits on. This 'borrowed scenery' makes the grounds of the house seemingly endless.

The design of the house is such that the side facing the golf course is virtually transparent so as to maximize the views from within the house. In keeping with the tropical design, this transparency is not achieved in the form of vast glass panels but rather sliding and folding doors, shutters and louvres which can all open up to allow natural ventilation through the house.

The plan is essentially two blocks joined by a stairwell which is expressed as a 'cage'. Its external walls are mostly porous panels of adjustable louvres in glass and timber. The staircase itself comprises flights of open risers to accentuate the lightness of the stairwell.

Recycled railway sleepers from old Malaysian railway tracks are used here extensively as paving on the ground, fence paneling as well as customized outdoor garden furniture.

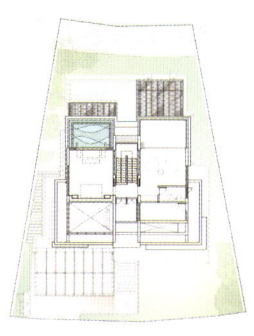

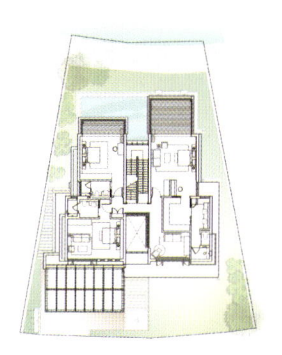

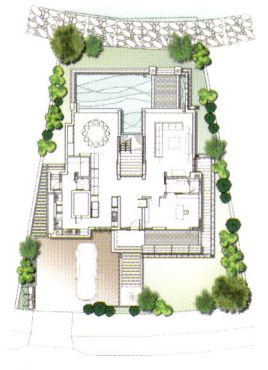

attic

second storey

first storey

Timeless Tropical

previous page dusk view of the front of the house. this house does not open out onto the sea or a waterway. instead, there is a small lake which separates the house from the sentosa golf course. *opposite page, far left* a full height panel of glass louvres opens up the house onto a view of the lake and golf course. *left* the front door of the house is preceded with a walkway made up of recycled railway sleepers from malaysian railway tracks. *right* the rear of the house also has large balconies with a view of the lake and golf course.

Sentosa Cove House Two

the stairwell located at the heart of the house is designed to be transparent in order to maintain visual connection to the waterway behind the house. *clockwise from left* view through the stairwell into the living room; the stairwell at ground level, the pebbled floor extends into the reflective pool beyond the glass panel; full height glass louvres seen from the second floor level; at the top of the stairwell, the space completely opens up via banks of timber louvres that serve as partitions to the rooms on both sides.

clockwise from above the living room opens out to the waterway outside; a small reflective pool acts as a safety barrier outside the attic tea-room. visually, this pool with an overflowing edge, appears to merge with the waterway behind the house; two views of the master bathroom.

Sentosa Cove House Three

Located on Sentosa Cove's waterway, this house is built for a family with two children. From the road, the house presents itself as a series of pitched roofs over an H-form with a solid first level façade and a light, almost transparent second level. The entry into the house is through a timber bridge that looks down into the basement courtyard.

Upon entering the house, one's view is drawn through the double-volume glass façade to the glass mosaic pool and to the canal waters beyond. The living and dining spaces extend into the outdoor pavilions and enclose part of the pool. The pavilions with big overhanging roofs become outdoor living spaces for the family regardless of the weather.

The central staircase draws one up to the second level and then to the attic. The same staircase also continues down to the basement. A chengal timber screen forms part of the staircase railing and accentuates the verticality of the double-volume space.

The attic contains the study and is bathed in light from all sides. It opens onto roof terraces, which wrap round the attic and provide views of the waterway on one side and glimpses of the sea on the other.

The master bedroom suite takes up one side of the H-block with a large bedroom that extends into a balcony overlooking the pool, the gym and the sea beyond. Tall vertical timber louvres line the length of the master bathroom and a skylight provides light for lush greenery to thrive in the bathroom planter. Three bedrooms occupy the other side of the H-block with similarly styled bathrooms.

The use of large roof overhangs and one-room wide spaces epitomize the essence of building forms in the tropics by providing shelter from the sun and rain whilst having openings on all sides to provide good cross-ventilation.

Materials such as bamboo and timber are used extensively. They provide a woody contrast to the background of natural stones, resulting in a rich, sensual palette.

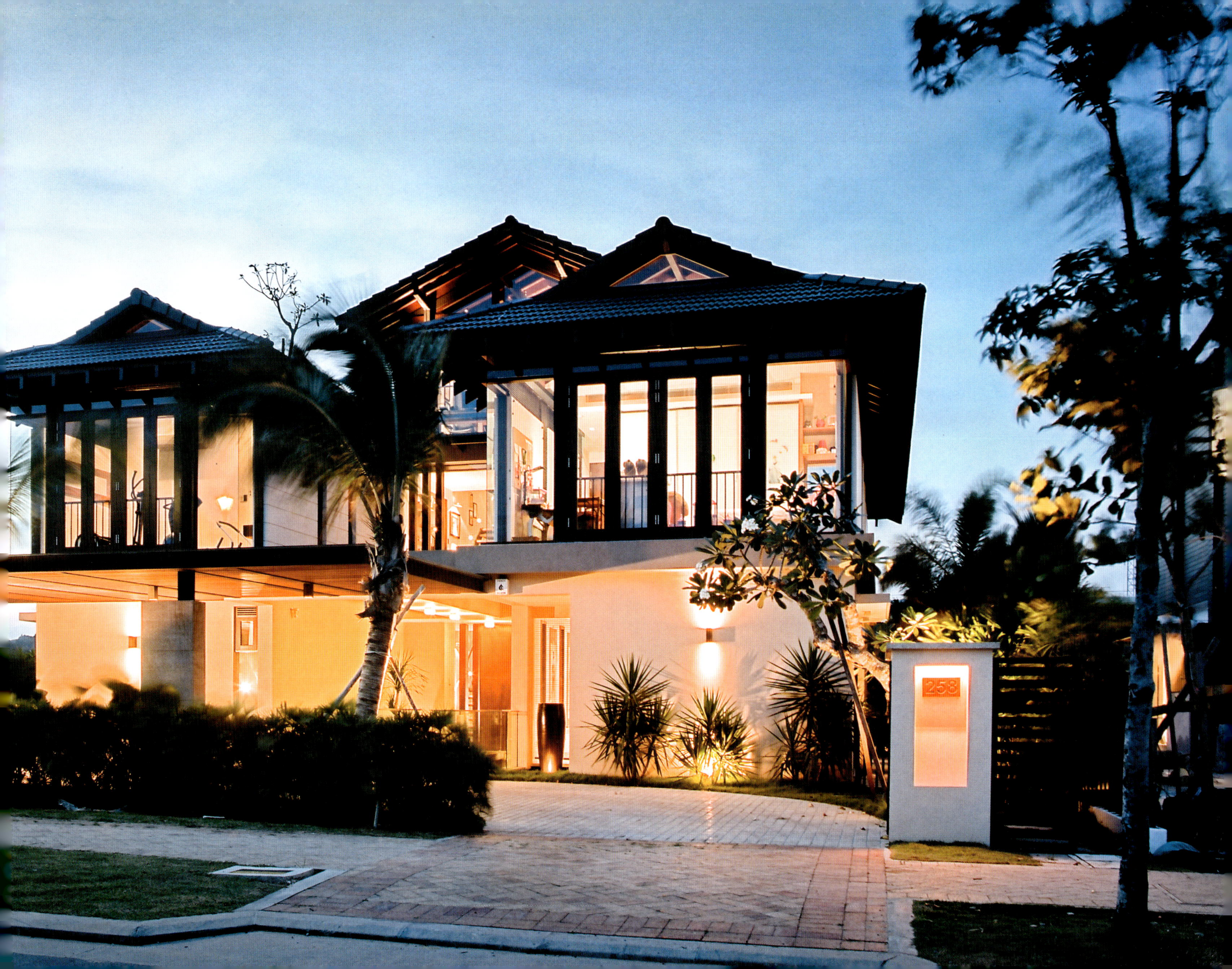
258

previous page the different layers of pitched roofs are accentuated by the lighting, creating a glow to the house at night. *left* view across the pool to the pavilions. *above* outdoor dining pavilion "floats" over the water. *opposite page* layering of spaces and roofs give the house more spatial depth.

second storey *first storey*

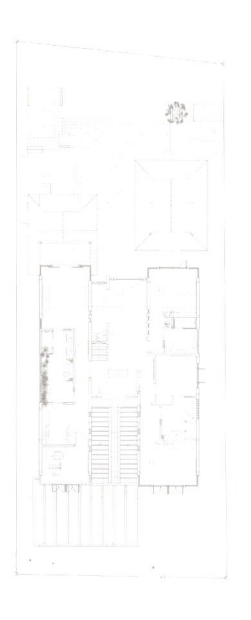

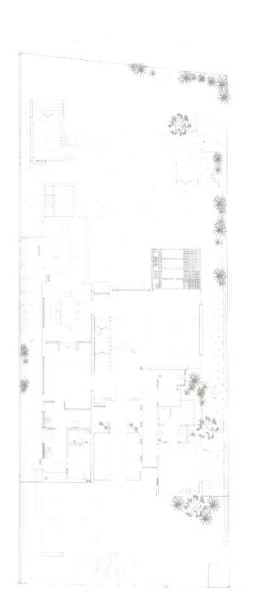

Sentosa Cove House Three | 097

Timeless Tropical

opposite page, left the staircase volume soars through the house connecting the basement up to the attic. timber screen accentuates the verticality of this space. *left* view from entrance towards the pool and waterway. *top and bottom* a cozy niche for working and looking out to the waters; living room extends to the garden. *right and far right* master bathroom has skylight over planter and vertical timber louvres.

Sentosa Cove House Three | 099

Sentosa Cove House Four

Capitalising on the wide frontage of this sea-facing site, the house is laid out in a staggered manner so as to maximise the views of the sea from almost all the rooms in this house.

The informal lifestyle of the owners, a family of five, allows for an open ground floor living space with transparency to the garden and the spacious expanse of the sea. The large pivot doors open out onto timber decks, thereby extending the living spaces onto the terraces and capturing the essence of living in the tropics. The timber terraces hug the pool and a pavilion at the far end forms a focal point in the garden. The pool is slightly elevated above the garden with water overflowing from a glass edge at the end, creating a seamless transition from the pool's blue glass tiles to the sea beyond.

The classic characteristics of a tropical house are incorporated here – large overhanging roof eaves and a deep balcony that runs along the sea-facing bedrooms on the second storey, both of which provide good sun and rain protection to the rooms whilst pivot doors again extend the bedroom spaces into the open.

101

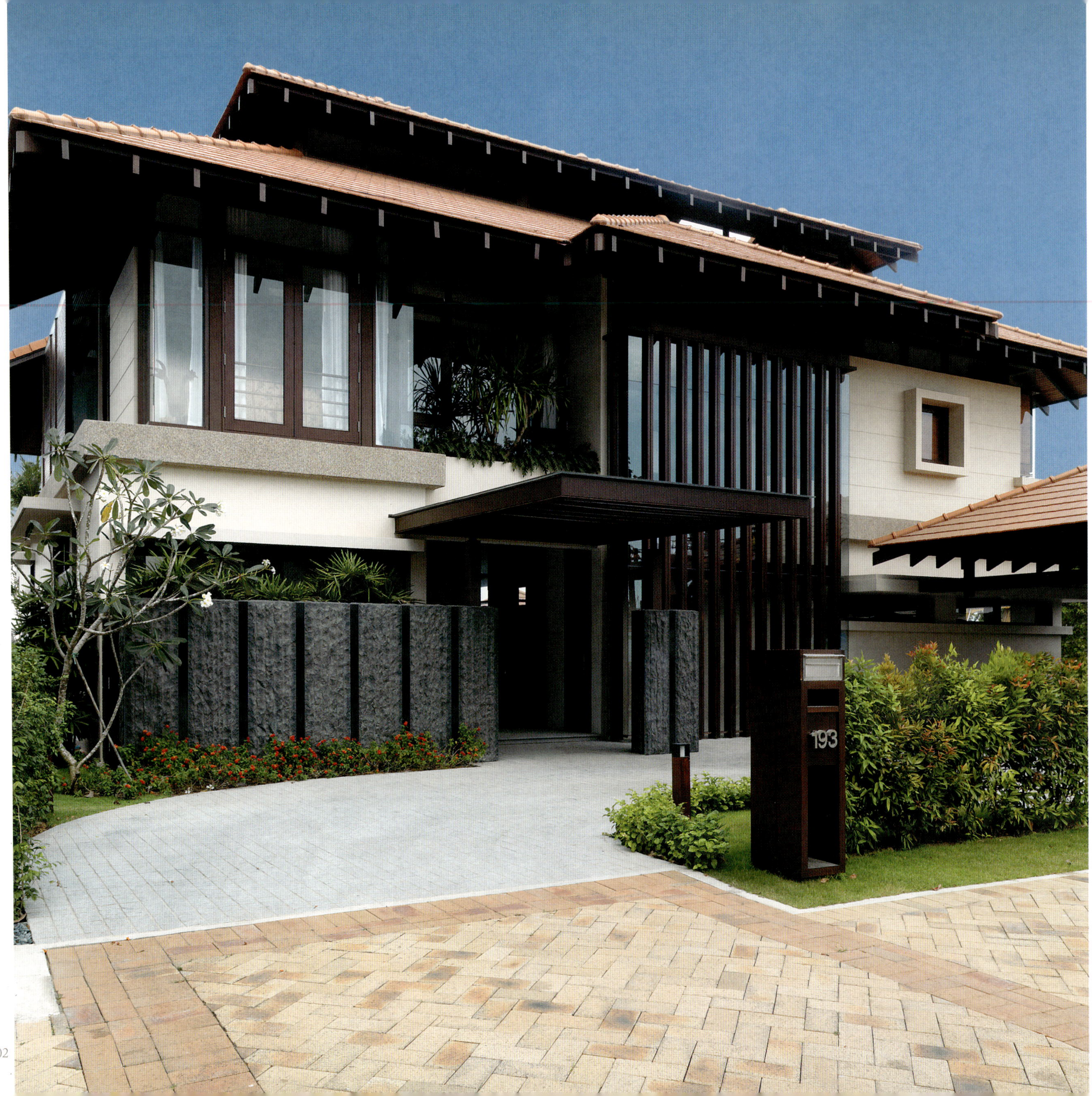
193

attic

second storey

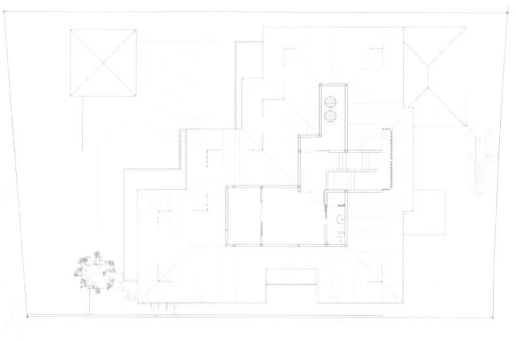

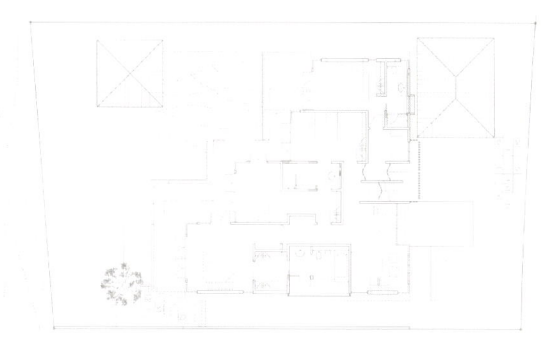

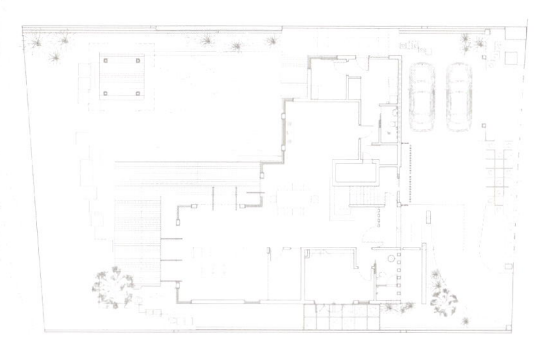

first storey

previous page balconies line the rooms on the sea-facing side of house.
opposite page large pitched roofs provide tropical shelter to the house.
right bedrooms open out onto balconies, thus extending the internal spaces.

left staircase volume is defined by timber framed glass panels. *top* living room opens onto timber decks. *bottom* master bathroom is bathed in natural light from skylight and screen. *opposite page* open kitchen has visual connection to the pool and garden.

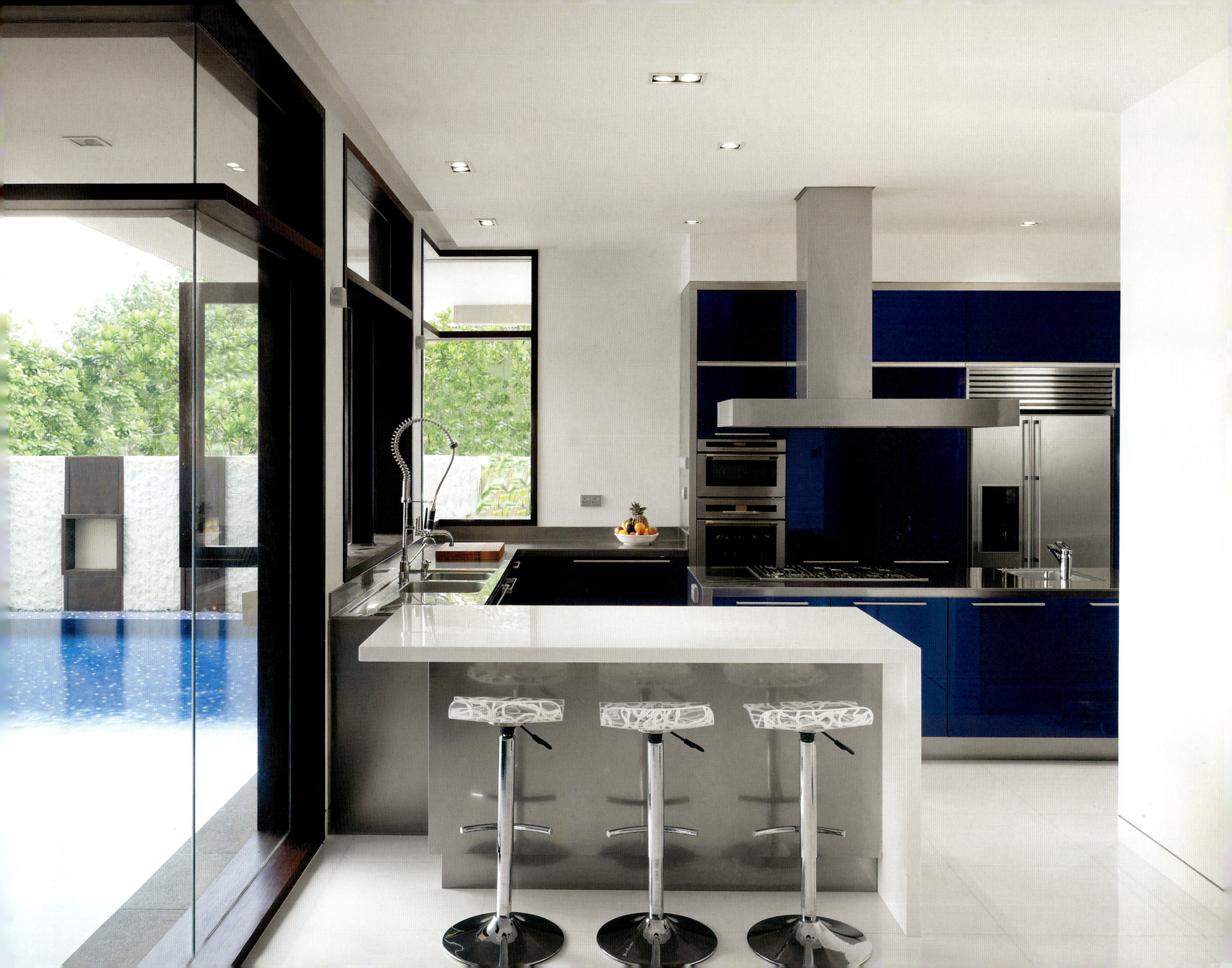

Sentosa Cove House Five

The unique hill slope locale of this house makes it stand out from the rest of the properties at Sentosa Cove.

Despite being within the Sentosa waterfront housing enclave, this is one of the few plots which is not adjacent to any water body – canal or sea. This is why the plot comes with a design guideline concession of an additional floor so as to have access to spectacular views of the city and Marina Bay.

The house is deliberately designed with tall and narrow proportions in order to accentuate the fact that it is one of the tallest bungalows in Sentosa Cove. Together with an "exposed" basement which houses the carporch, the house is five levels high. The master bedroom is located on the highest attic level as it has the most commanding views of the sea from such a vantage point. The entire front of the house is made of timber balconies that cantilever off like three-dimensional wooden screens.

The main living spaces of the house are located one level up, accessed by two sets of staircases. The spaces are designed to be totally porous; with the living and dining pavilions totally unenclosed. These interior spaces open into the pool and deck area and are followed all the way through to the natural slope of the hill, creating a valley-like central oasis. All the bedrooms on the upper levels also open up onto this vista.

The design of this house demonstrates authentic tropical living that strongly focuses on the relationship between the interior spaces and their surroundings. The colossal matured trees rising from the upper part of the hill slope complete this picturesque setting.

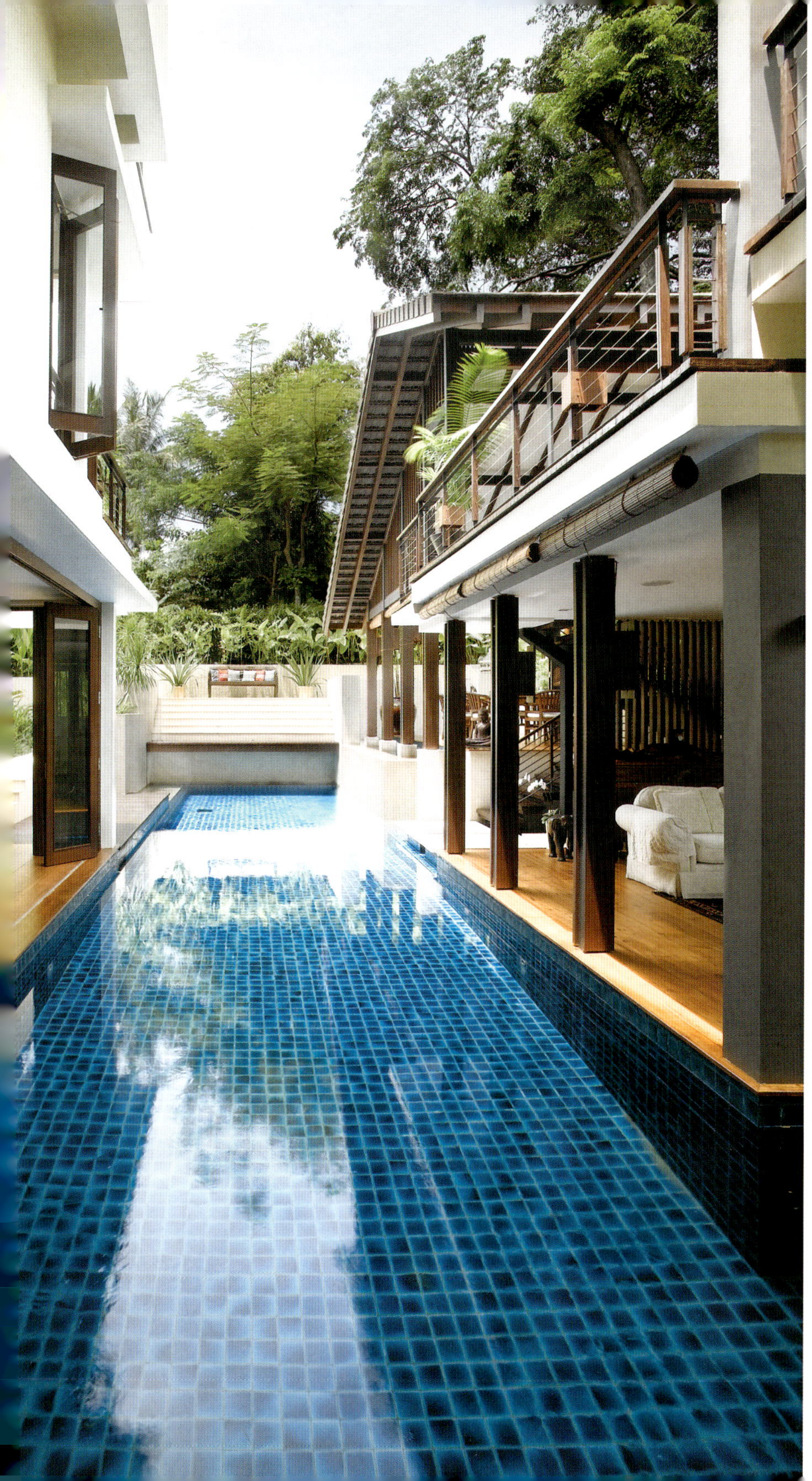

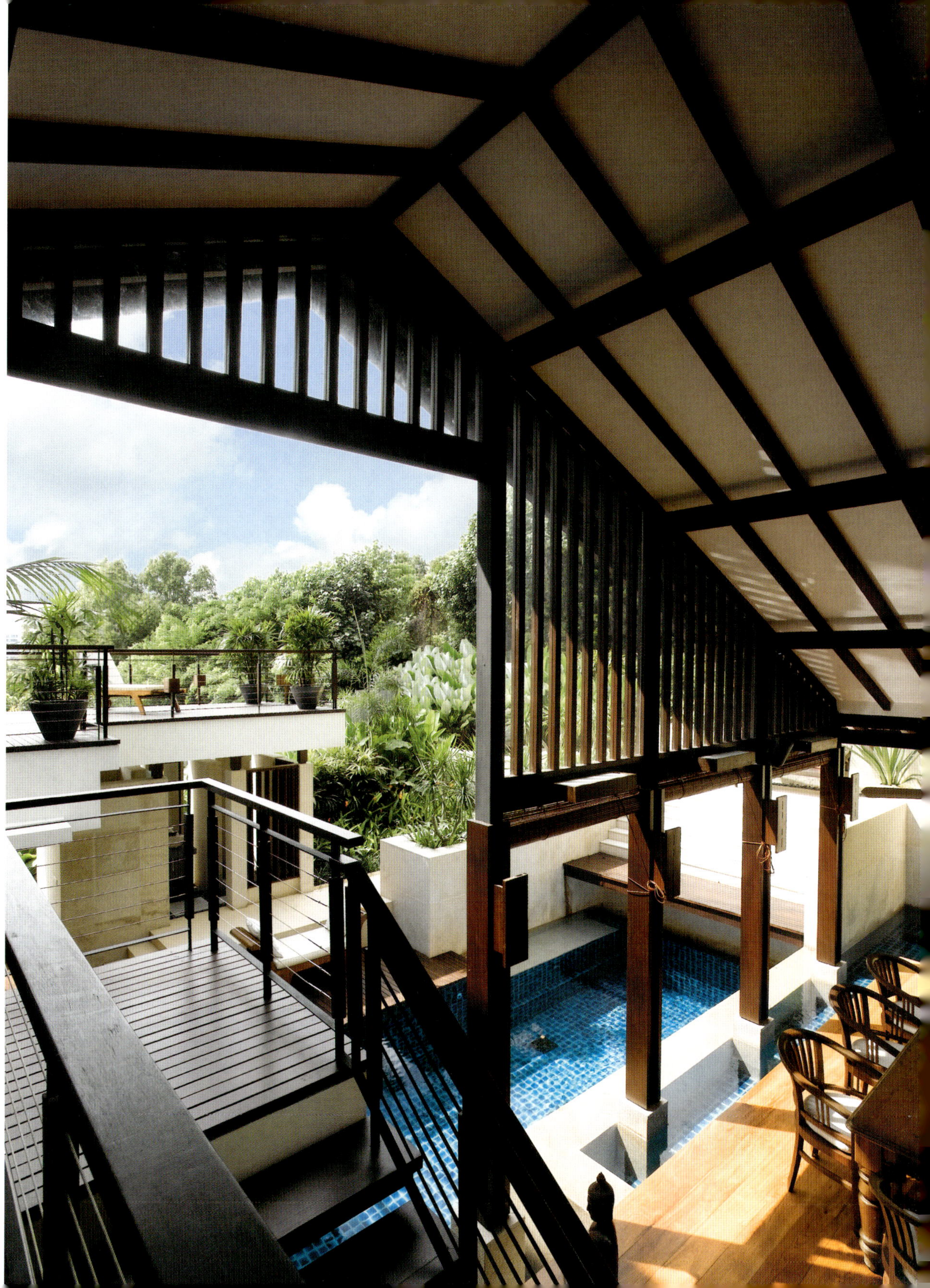

Timeless Tropical

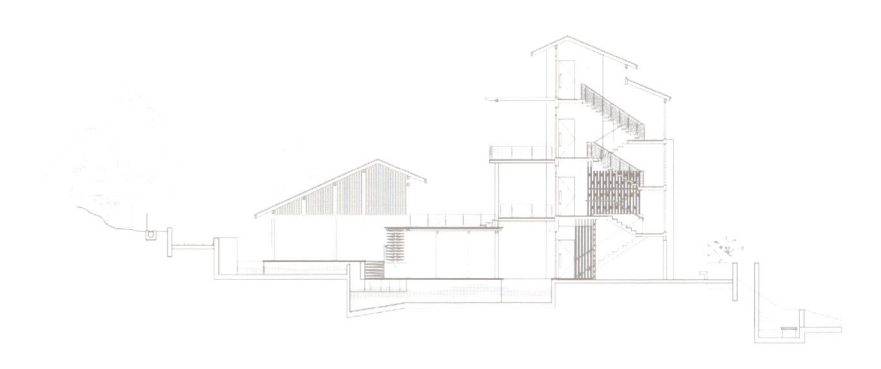

previous page, left to right linear swimming pool sandwiched in between the two wings. the family room on the left and the dining pavilion both open directly onto the pool; the open-sided dining pavilion beside the swimming pool. *opposite page, far left* side elevation of the house. the form tapers from the main house down to the open-sided dining pavilion. *top* front of the house which cuts into the existing hill slope. *bottom* close-up view of the front balconies. *section drawing* of the house indicates how it cuts into the existing hill slope. *right* view of the house from the high point of the hill slope, looking down to the linear swimming pool.

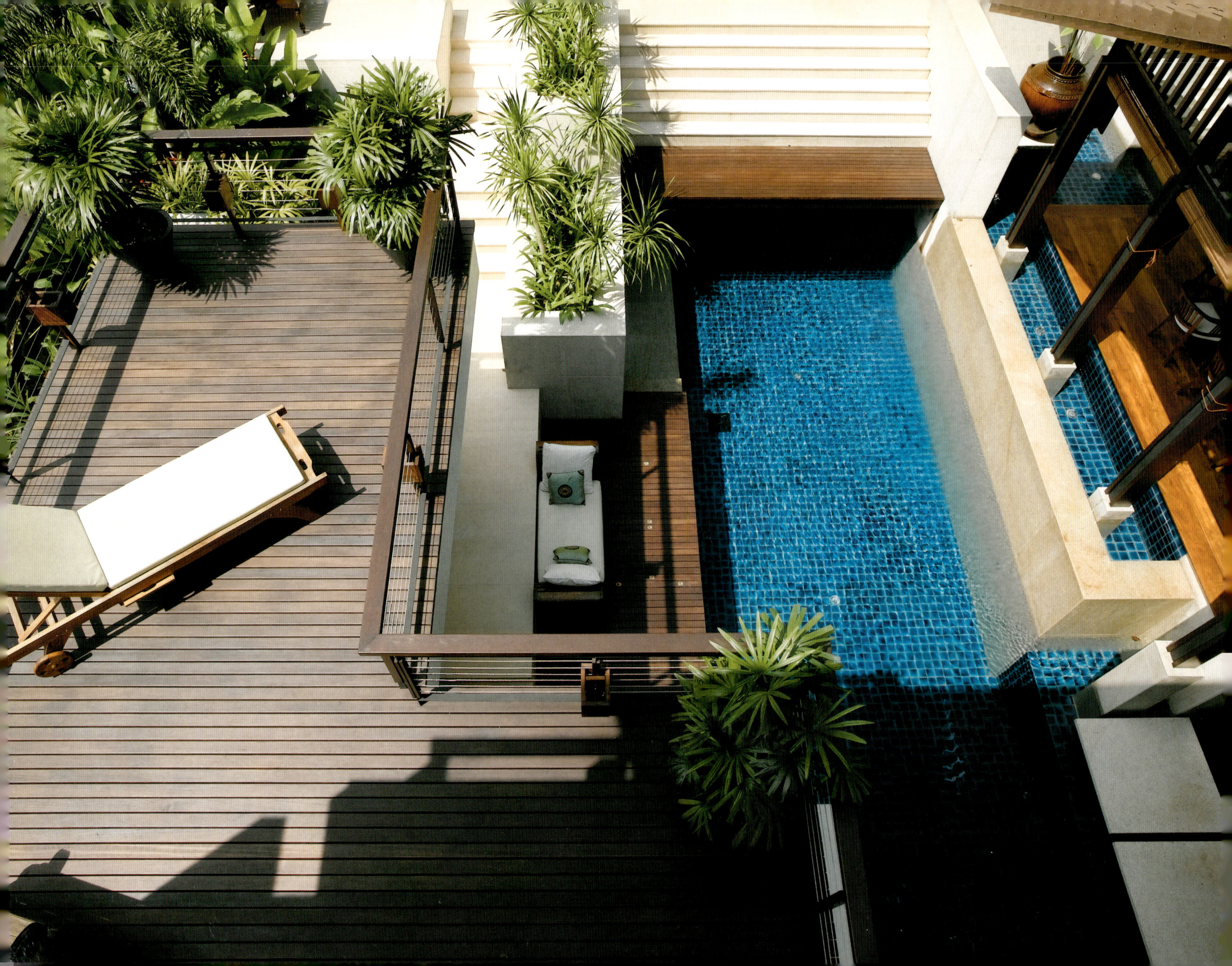

opposite page timber decks at various levels all look into the swimming pool at the centre of the house. *right* stepping stones and stairs to the dining pavilion, an open-ended semi-outdoor space that keeps in line with the tropical theme.

Sentosa Cove House Five | 111

Timeless Tropical

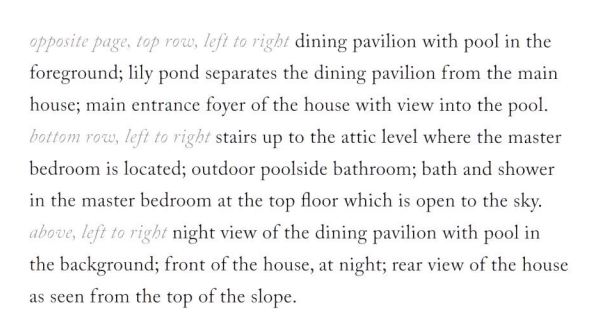

opposite page, top row, left to right dining pavilion with pool in the foreground; lily pond separates the dining pavilion from the main house; main entrance foyer of the house with view into the pool.
bottom row, left to right stairs up to the attic level where the master bedroom is located; outdoor poolside bathroom; bath and shower in the master bedroom at the top floor which is open to the sky.
above, left to right night view of the dining pavilion with pool in the background; front of the house, at night; rear view of the house as seen from the top of the slope.

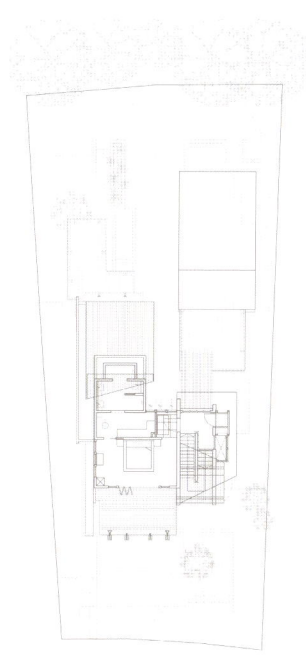

attic storey 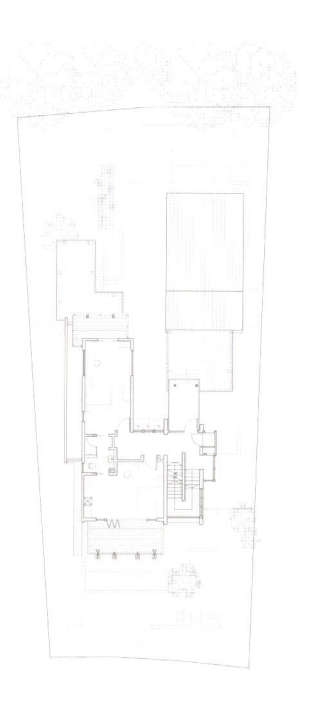 *third storey* 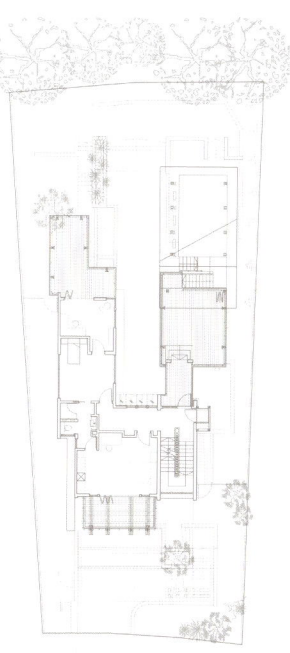 *second storey* 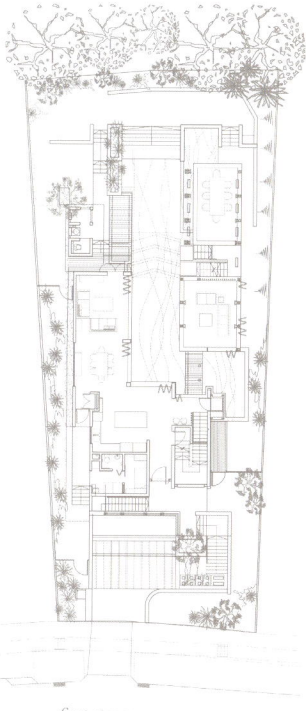 *first storey*

Sentosa Cove House Five | 113

Beachfront Facilities at Palawan Beach, Sentosa

The small island of Sentosa was formerly a military fort during the British colonial era in Singapore. Today, it is a famous leisure destination. Palawan Beach, located at the southern-most point of the island and built mostly on reclaimed land, is where a hub of leisure-oriented facilities are situated.

Built on a partially manmade beach setting, the central cluster is dedicated to family and children and its facilities range from food outlets, shops and activity areas. The latter includes an amphitheatre for staging animal shows and an outdoor waterplay area that incorporates two original defence bunkers from Sentosa's days as a fort that have been repainted as evocative eye-catching sculptures.

The planning of this hub adopts a casual approach, allowing the open beach to merge into sheltered yet unenclosed spaces. In keeping with true tropical living, there is little delineation between what is inside and what is outside.

The architecture here is unassuming. Balancing contemporary clean-line expression with the vernacular, the buildings are designed to grow out and evolve naturally from its settings. This can be seen in the timber decks merging with sandy beaches, trees growing through roof trellises, toilets opening onto the landscape and the plumbing for the shower heads which are embedded within coconut tree trunks.

Judging by the popularity of this beach hub, it is apparent that the built product has fully met the requirements of the design brief which called for architecture that complements the spaces in between rather than drawing attention to itself.

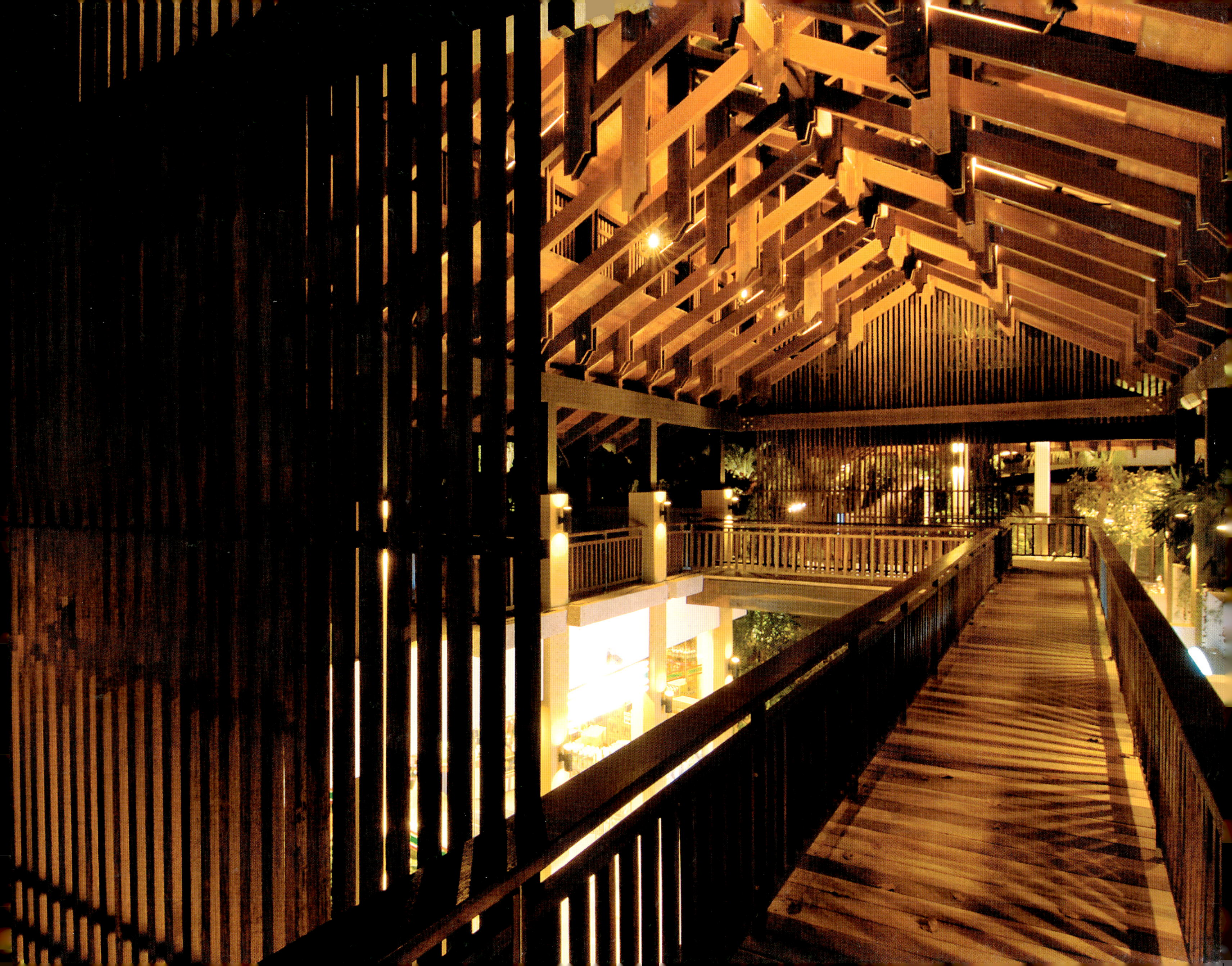

116 | Timeless Tropical

previous page night view of main covered public gathering space which acts as a meeting point for the various beach-front facilities. *opposite page* daytime views of the main gathering space. *right* covered linkway to the cafeteria; coconut trunks used as columns and bintangor branches serve as handrails. bamboo chick blinds are used for sun shading on the timber trellis roof.

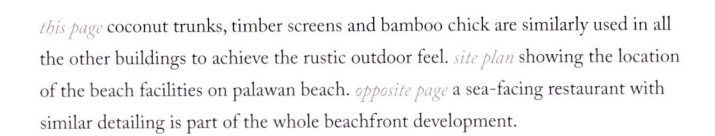

this page coconut trunks, timber screens and bamboo chick are similarly used in all the other buildings to achieve the rustic outdoor feel. *site plan* showing the location of the beach facilities on palawan beach. *opposite page* a sea-facing restaurant with similar detailing is part of the whole beachfront development.

118 | Timeless Tropical

Beachfront Facilities at Palawan Beach, Sentosa | 119

120 | Timeless Tropical

opposite page, clockwise from top left coconut trunks, timber screens and bamboo chick are also used in all the other buildings to achieve the rustic outdoor feel. *above and right* the skylight over the main gathering space, day and night views.

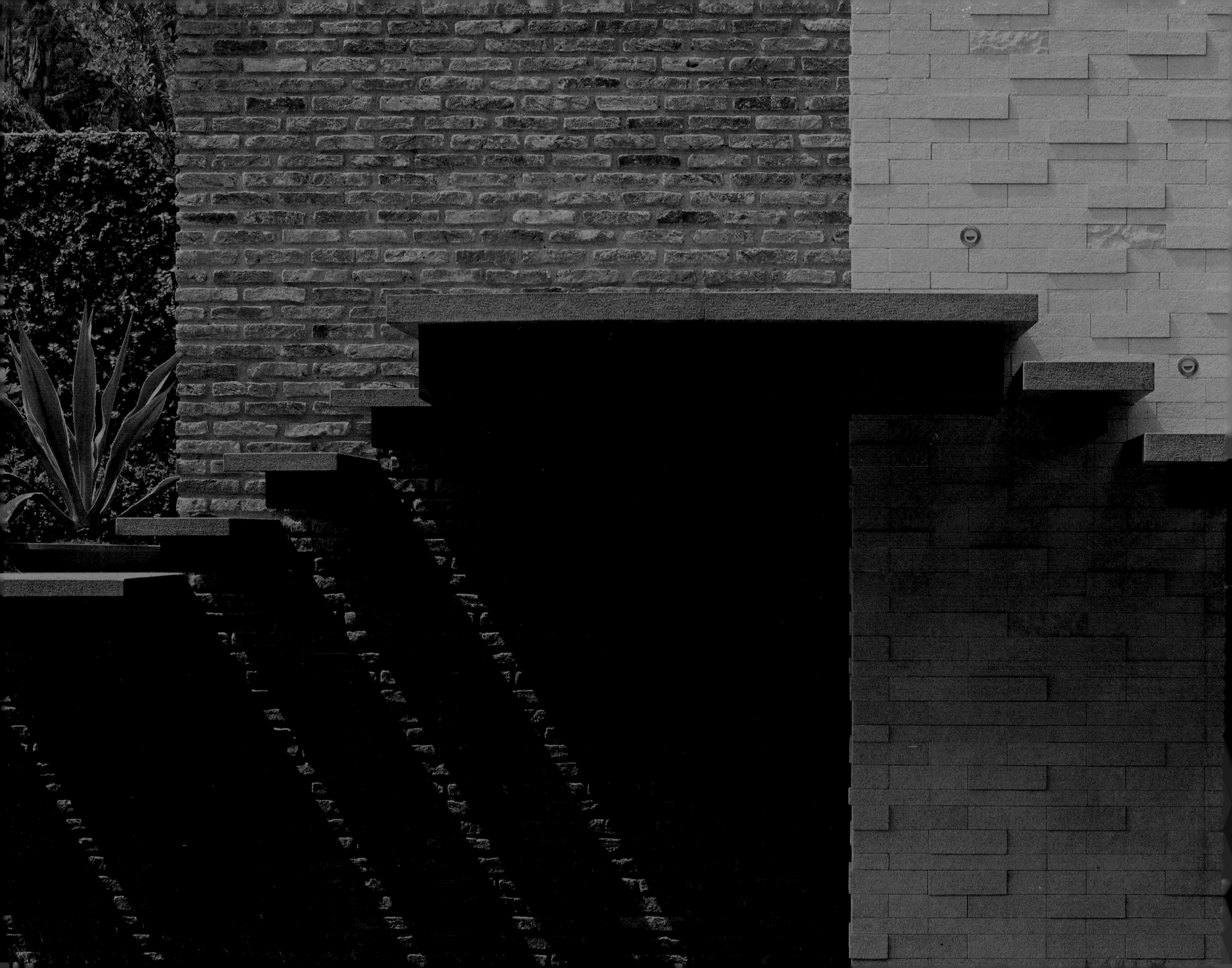

Appendix

Other Projects

HOUSES | 1991-1995

Terrace house at Jalan Mas Kuning
Semi-detached house at Mt Sinai Avenue
Semi-detached house at Eng Kong Garden
Terrace house at Cheng Soon Garden
2 semi-detached houses at Jalan Pelatok
Conservation shophouse at Emerald Hill Road
Terrace house at Taman Mas Merah
2 units shop/office at Outram Road
2 terrace houses at Jalan Lakum
Semi-detached house at Sunbird Avenue
Terrace house at Cairnhill Circle
Terrace house at Kingswear Avenue
2 semi-detached houses at Zehnder Road
Semi-detached house at Namly Drive
Semi-detached house at Taman Siglap
Terrace house at Siglap Road

1996-1999

2002-2005

Detached house at Jalan Lateh
Semi-detached house at Coronation Road West
2 semi-detached and 2 detached houses at Saraca Hill
Terrace house One at Makepeace Road (1993)
Semi-detached house at Vanda Crescent
Conservation Bungalow at Nassim Road
Detached house at Hua Guan Avenue
Detached house at Victoria Park Close
Semi-detached house at Hua Guan Avenue
Detached house at Oriole Crescent
Detached house at Sunset Square
Semi-detached house at Poh Huat Road
Detached house at Berrima Road
Terrace house Two at Makepeace Road
Semi-detached house at Greenleaf Drive
Semi-detached house at Crowhurst Drive
Detached house at Siglap Bank
Detached house at Tanglin Hill

124 | Timeless Tropical

2006-2009

Terrace house at Gelang Patah, Johor
Detached house at Sunset Avenue
Detached house at Jalan Sejarah
Terrace house at Jalan Tari Serimpi
Detached house at Jasmine Road
Semi-detached house at Goldhill Avenue
Detached house at Ramsgate Road
Terrace house at Kismis Avenue
Detached house at Pinewood Grove
Semi-detached house at Ascot Rise
Detached house at Victoria Park Road
2 detached houses at Heng Mui Keng Terrace
Semi-detached house at Jalan Seni
Semi-detached house at Jalan Kebaya
Semi-detached house at East Coast Terrace
6 units of waterfront terrace houses at Sentosa Cove

Semi-detached house at Meyer Road
Semi-detached house at Mt Sinai Plain
3 pairs of semi-detached houses at Boscombe Road
Golf Villas at Emirates Premier Club, Abu Dhabi, UAE
4 detached houses One at Goodman Road
2 pairs of semi-detached houses at Jalan Ampang
Detached house at Broadrick Road
Detached house Two at Mt Echo Park
Detached waterfront house at Sentosa Cove

Other Projects | 125

2006-2009

Semi-detached house at Jalan Baiduri
Conservation shophouse at Amoy Street
Detached house at Frankel Walk
Detached house in Yangon, Myanmar
Detached house at Jalan Pisang Emas
Semi-detached house at Clementi Crescent
4 detached houses Two at Goodman Road

NON-RESIDENTIAL

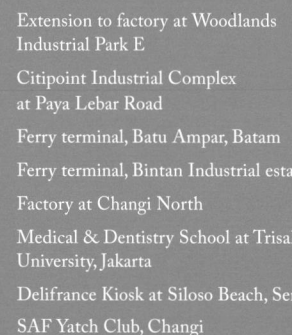

Extension to factory at Woodlands Industrial Park E
Citipoint Industrial Complex at Paya Lebar Road
Ferry terminal, Batu Ampar, Batam
Ferry terminal, Bintan Industrial estate
Factory at Changi North
Medical & Dentistry School at Trisakti University, Jakarta
Delifrance Kiosk at Siloso Beach, Sentosa
SAF Yatch Club, Changi
Commercial/Apartment Block at Race Course Road
Hillview Park Connector from Bukit Batok Nature Park to Bukit Batok Town Park
Visitors' Centre & Facilities for Eco-tourism in Sentosa

INTERIORS

Apartment at Mt Elizabeth Towers
Semi-detached house at St Helier's Avenue
Detached house at Neram Road
Detached house at Fifth Avenue
Cafe restaurant at Far East Square
Cafe restaurant at Temasek Tower
Maisonnette apartment at Chatsworth Court
Office at Pidemco Centre
Dialysis Centre at Strathmore Avenue
Office at Outram Road
Semi-detached house at Ming Teck Park
Clinic at Mt Elizabeth Medical Centre
Detached house One at Harlyn Road
Detached house Two at Harlyn Road
O&G Specialist Clinic at National University Hospital
Office at Unity Towers
Restaurant, Century Square
Restaurant, Jurong Point
Show flat at Meadowlodge
Apartment at Nassim Hill
Home Nursing Foundation Headquarters, Toa Payoh
Maisonette apartment at Balmoral Road
METTA Welfare Association Headquarters Building at Simei Street 1
Cafe Restaurant at OUB Centre
Cafe Restaurant at ICON Village
University Surgical Centre, National University Hospital

126 | Timeless Tropical

Timur Designs

The publication of *Timeless Tropical* would not have been possible if not for the generosity of the home owners who have graciously allowed us to intrude upon the privacy of their homes to take all the photographs featured in this monograph.

For that, we sincerely thank Hsin-Li and Danny, Regina and Martin, Adeline and Leslie, Chris and John, the Liew family, Lily and Robert, Annabel and Neil, Mr and Mrs Tay, Susan and Peter, Sharon and Mark, Michelle and Dale as well as the Sentosa Development Corporation. We also thank the owners of all other projects that Timur Designs has undertaken since its inception in 1991, which could not be included in this publication due to limitation of space.

We most certainly have not forgotten all those who have contributed in the past, to all the works we have done: Ong Hui Hoon, Benson Ang Koon Guan, Chua Kien Hoong, Aznizah Aris, Yeo Kwang Teck, Derrick Tan Wei San, Mark Chee Lip Wui, Kenneth Chia Kok Keong, Sufian Supa'at, Mohamad Noor, Kenneth Tan Chong Hwee, Lee Teng Kwee and Rawiwan Vithyakomol.

And of course, the architect never works alone. We have to thank the teams of consultants who have worked with us to transform our initial paper sketches and cardboard models into the buildings which are featured here: Structural Engineers – WTS Consulting Engineers, CSE Consultants, Mott MacDonald Singapore Pte Ltd, NCK Associates; Mechanical & Electrical Engineers – GIMS & Associates, P Tan & Partners, Technocon Engineers Pte Ltd; Quantity Surveyors – RJ Consultants Pte Ltd; Landscape Consultants – ICN Design International, as well as SPECS Consultants.

For everyone who contributed to the making of this publication, we extend our gratitude – Joanne and her team at ORO *editions*, the photographers Tim Nolan, Maurice Lee and Edward Hendricks, Diane Tan for painstakingly selecting all the photographs, Dr Wong Yunn Chii for your insightful foreword and Eddy Koh of Heart Publishing for editing our texts and for suggesting the idea of doing this monograph.

And finally, to all those still toiling away with us to continue creating more wonderful architecture to feature in our next publication – Md Jufri b Md Yusoff, Diane Tan Mei-yin, Lim Meng Kuan, William Lim Guan Hui and Jasmine Yue Bee Luan – our heartfelt appreciation for all the long hours contributed towards all these projects.

Yong Ai Loon
Chan Wai Kin

PHOTO CREDITS

Tim Nolan:
Cover, 002, 004, 006, 009, 022, 023 *top left, middle right and bottom left*, 024-026, 027 *top row*, 028-037, 038 *bottom*, 039-061, 068-079, 088-099, 114-123.

Maurice Lee:
010-011, 012 *right*, 013, 014-019, 020 *except bottom row, centre*, 021 *bottom row*, 080 *except top right*, 081-087, 106 *except top right and bottom right*, 107-112.

Edward Hendricks:
062-065, 067, 100-105.

Chan Wai Kin:
012 *first four from left*, 020 *bottom row, centre*, 021 *top row*, 023 *top right, middle left and bottom right*, 027 *bottom*, 106 *top right and bottom right*, 113.

Diane Tan Mei-yin:
066.

Tim Nolan is a British photographer who has been based in Singapore since 1993. His work includes architectural and interiors photography for a variety of international clients. His photographs have been featured in magazines and books published in Singapore and around the world. He also produces photographic and digital artworks for corporate clients. www.timnolanphoto.com.

If the eyes are windows to one's soul, then *Maurice Lee's* lens is an aperture to a kaleidoscope of breathtaking possibilities. With film as his canvas, he believes in imbuing everyday objects with fresh excitement and curiosity that captures your imagination and takes you to a different world. www.mauricecolorbox.com.

Edward Hendricks has been a successful professional photographer for over 18 years. He specializes in interiors, architecture, still life and profiles of people. His work has appeared internationally and in the region's design and lifestyle publications. ciaphoto@singnet.com.sg

COPYRIGHT

ORO *editions*
Publishers of Architecture, Art, and Design
Gordon Goff – Publisher
USA: PO Box 998, Pt Reyes Station, CA 94956
Asia: Block 8, Lorong Bakar Batu #02-04, Singapore 348743
www.oroeditions.com
info@oroeditions.com

Copyright © 2010 by ORO *editions*

ISBN: 978-0-9820607-9-7

Designed and Produced by ORO *editions* Pte Ltd, Singapore
Graphic Design: Andrés Rodríguez and Davina Tjandra
Copy Editing: Melanie Lee
Project and Production Manager: Joanne Tan
Color Separation and Printing: ORO *group* Ltd
Text printed using offset sheetfed printing process in 5 color on 157gsm premium matt art paper with an off-line gloss spot varnish applied to all photographs.

All rights reserved. No part of this book may be reproduced, stored in a retrieval system, or transmitted in any form or by any means, including electronic, mechanical, photocopying of microfilming, recording, or otherwise (except that copying permitted by Sections 107 and 108 of the U.S. Copyright Law and except by reviewers for the public press) without written permission from the publisher.

ORO *editions* has made every effort to minimize the carbon footprint of this project. In pursuit of this goal, ORO *editions*, in association with Global ReLeaf, has arranged to plant two trees for each and every tree used in the manufacturing of the FSC paper produced for this book. Global ReLeaf is an international campaign run by American Forests, the nation's oldest nonprofit conservation organization. Global ReLeaf is American Forests' education and action program that helps individuals, organizations, agencies, and corporations improve the local and global environment by planting and caring for trees.

North American and International Distribution:
Publishers Group West
1700 Fourth Street
Berkeley, CA 94710
USA
www.pgw.com